CLASSROOM MANAGEMENT WITH ADOLESCENTS

Edited by

James D. Long
Appalachian State University

Robert L. Williams
University of Tennessee

MSS Information Corporation
655 Madison Avenue, New York, N.Y. 10021

This is a custom-made book of readings prepared for the courses taught by the editors, as well as for related courses and for college and university libraries. For information about our program, please write to:

MSS INFORMATION CORPORATION
655 Madison Avenue
New York, New York 10021

MSS wishes to express its appreciation to the authors of the articles in this collection for their cooperation in making their work available in this format.

Library of Congress Cataloging in Publication Data

Long, James D   1942-   comp.
    Classroom management with adolescents.

    1. Classroom management--Addresses, essays, lectures.
2. Adolescence--Addresses, essays, lectures.
I. Williams, Robert L., 1937-   joint comp.
II. Title.
LB3011.L58   373.1'1'02   73-3077
ISBN 0-8422-0288-9

CONTENTS

With the plethora of books now being published in the area of classroom management, why another one? One doesn't have to be the paragon of erudition to know that quantity is not always positively correlated with quality. The most interminable lecture may contain zero substance. Similarly, a multiplicity of books on classroom management does not necessarily mean adequate coverage. In fact, there are some horrendous gaps in the behavior modification literature. None is more apparent than the application of behavior management procedures to adolescent populations, particularly adolescents in regular classroom settings. Literally hundreds of studies describe the use of operant procedures with kindergarten and primary age children; only a handful investigate the utility of such procedures with adolescents. The present book brings together most of these adolescent-behavior management studies. By "adolescents," we mean students of junior and senior high school age.

The issues covered in this book are considered important not only by behavior modifiers but by educators of vastly different persuasions. To give you a context in which to consider these "titillating" issues, we have initially included a brief overview of how behavior modification can be applied to adolescents. This overview, "A Model for Influencing Adolescents' Behavior," should sharpen your ability to evaluate the specific applications of behavior management principles included in the remainder of the book.

The first major section of the book deals with the possibility of self-management by adolescents. Critics of behavior modification have been quite concerned about the extent to which the source of behavioral control is external to the student. Ideally, the student should learn to control his own contingencies, supply his own setting events, and produce his own rewards and punishments. The studies included in Section One will describe the logistics for achieving these auspicious possibilities. The section on contingency contracting (Section Two) also places heavy emphasis on student involvement in the determination of classroom objectives and the avenues for reaching those objectives. You should be particularly alert to the respective roles of teachers and students under a contracting system. Section Two will also indicate the comparative effectiveness of contracts with different types of high school populations.

Section Three investigates the possibility of modifying adolescents' behavior via teacher attention. You will be interested to learn that teacher attention has much the same effects during adolescence as it does during early and middle childhood. It seems that adolescents have not outgrown their need to be seen, heard, and approved.

The last two sections of the book attempt to appraise the impact of operant procedures on academic performance and social problems. Most behavior management studies have dealt with

classroom conduct, not academic achievement. The first study
in Section Four focuses on the correlation between classroom
social conduct and academic performance. Other studies in
Section Four elucidate the efficacy of operant procedures
when applied directly to academic indices. The impact of
behavior management procedures on basic societal problems
is explored in Section Five. We refer to problems such as
inter-racial relationships, environmental pollution, over-
population, drug abuse, and international conflict. Very few
behavior modification studies have dealt with such profound
issues. However, we hope that the studies included in Section
Five will be an impetus for additional operant research of
that type.

Hopefully, you will find most of the articles in this
book enjoyable and understandable. If you encounter difficulty, it will likely be in the "Results" sections of certain
articles. If any statistical analysis transcends your present
background in experimental design, skip the "Results" section
of that article and go directly to the "Discussion" section.
The "Discussion" section will usually tell you in non-
statistical terms what the findings of the study were and
the implications of those findings. If you have an acute
interest in techniques for training teachers to use behavior
management strategies or procedures for recording classroom
behaviors, examine closely the "Method" sections of the various
articles. Whatever your particular reason for exploring the
content of this book, have fun!

A MODEL FOR INFLUENCING ADOLESCENTS' BEHAVIOR

James D. Long   Robert L. Williams
Appalachian State University   University of Tennessee

Adolescence is often characterized as a time of "storm and stress," a period in which youths rebel against authority, encounter excruciating parent-peer conflicts, and are driven by powerful biological forces. Such conceptions are not without question, however. Albert Bandura (1964), for example, contends that overinterpreting superficial signs (e.g., fads) of nonconformity, mass media sensationalizing of "typical" adolescent turmoil in order to sell copy, and generalizing from the behavior of deviant adolescents are the primary culprits responsible for perpetuating the adolescent mythology. Furthermore, Bandura suggests that adolescent sexual behavior is largely a result of social conditioning, not endocrinal stimulation.

Regardless of the position an individual may take with respect to adolescent development, agreement can be reached on several points. First, adolescents do have problems which, if unresolved, become magnified with increasing age. The adolescent who cannot read, who cannot get along with his peers, or who lacks other academic and social skills is likely to become the school dropout, the alienated youth, or eventually the unemployed adult. The adolescent years frequently represent the last chance for persons to acquire competencies needed for successful living. Certainly this period represents the last opportunity of the public schools to rectify any earlier failure on its part. Second, everyone would agree that, although adolescents have problems, adolescent behaviors can be influenced. In brief, adolescents with problems can be helped. The present article focuses on this second possibility. The major objective of the article is to provide a conceptual model for working with adolescents. The succeeding articles in the text fit within this model, providing explicit procedures for resolving a variety of adolescent problems.

Learning from Consequences

Basic to the model presented here is the premise that the overwhelming majority of human behavior (the only exception being reflexive behavior) is the result of learning. Young children, adolescents, and mature adults try out many behaviors; that is, they attempt to determine what consequences different actions will produce. In a sense, all human beings test their environments. This is particularly true of adolescents since environmental reactions to certain of their behaviors may be dramatically different from previous reactions. So it takes a great deal of environmental testing for the adolescent to determine current behavioral contingencies. By behavioral contingencies, we refer

ORIGINAL MANUSCRIPT, 1972.

to relationships between behaviors and the consequences produced by those behaviors. Behaviors which produce pleasant consequences tend to recur, whereas behaviors that have no effect on the environment or yield unpleasant consequences are dropped. In other words, a person learns to perform both good and bad behaviors because of the consequences produced by the behaviors.

Obviously, proper control of consequences could have a profound effect upon the behavior a person exhibits. What, for example, would be the result if significant adults (e.g., teachers, counselors, parents) arranged for pleasant consequences (e.g., attention, recognition, special privileges, success feedback) to follow appropriate adolescent behavior? High rates of appropriate behavior, no doubt. Unfortunately, consequences are often improperly managed. Some significant adults fail to recognize desirable behavior when it occurs, others follow practically any behavior with pleasant consequences, some attend only to negative behaviors, and still others are not consistent enough for youngsters to know what to expect. The results may range from adolescents who resort to delinquent behavior to gain recognition, to those who expect everything for nothing, to adolescents who have no conception of what constitutes right and wrong. Working with adolescents in a facilitative fashion is primarily a matter of effective consequence management.

Managing Consequences

The judicious control of consequences for adolescent behaviors is no simple undertaking. A strong emotional commitment and a plan of action will be necessary. The following steps are suggested as a plan for consequence control. The commitment to implement that plan must come from you.

Identify the Behaviors

The first step in controlling consequences is the proper identification of the behaviors to be influenced. The key here is specificity. Suppose a teacher identifies "poor student attitudes" as the major source of difficulty between herself and her students. The teacher is undoubtedly using "poor student attitude" as a shorthand description of the students' reactions. Shorthand labels are acceptable only so long as others know what they represent. More frequently than not, shorthand descriptions are open to many interpretations. For one teacher, "poor student attitude" may mean that students argue back when called down. For another teacher, "poor student attitude" may indicate that students are absent frequently, talk during study time, or fail to complete assignments. Even if teachers could agree on what "poor student attitude" means, a student might be hard pressed to understand the problem. Furthermore, labeling a student as having a poor attitude or as being stupid implies that something is wrong with the whole person. A better procedure is to pinpoint precise behaviors that are of concern. A precise behavior would be something which can be observed or measured directly. "Poor student attitude" refers more to an unobservable, internal state than to overt responses. Granted that a student's attitude may evidence itself in numerous overt behaviors. In that case, simply specify, observe, and measure those behaviors. The number of times a student talks back, attends to lessons, and completes assignments can be counted (i.e., measured directly). Thus, pinpointing behaviors circumvents the misinterpretations propagated by global attitudinal labels and prevents adolescents from acquiring stigmas attached to such labels.

Find Out Why

Determining why an adolescent behaves as he does is a simplier process following the precise identification of the problem behavior. For example, finding the consequences which control "arguing back when called down" would certainly be easier than determining the controlling consequences for a "poor attitude." Identifying the consequences controlling a specific behavior is further simplified by asking, "What does the individual receive as a result of his actions?" This question invariably supplies the answer as to why the person behaves as he does. For example, what usually happens when a youth misbehaves in class or gets into trouble with the law? He receives attention, a lot of it. Admittedly, this attention may be in the form of reprimands or even punishment, but others have at least been forced to respond to the youth. Furthermore, whether a consequence is pleasant or not is a function of the receiver's perception. It may be preferable to an adolescent to receive physical punishment for misbehavior than to be completely ignored for doing what is expected. Inappropriate conduct, of course, sometimes brings very pleasant consequences (e.g., rewards from parents for the youth's promise to do better, a two-week holiday suspension from school). The point is that an individual acts to produce consequences from the environment. Once the consequences controlling a behavior have been clearly established, steps can be undertaken to produce desirable behavior changes.

Make Appropriate Behavior Pay

Producing desirable behavior changes primarily involves two steps. First, the consequences that are controlling unwanted behavior must be withheld. If an adolescent is verbally abusing his teacher in order to receive attention, teacher attention following verbal abuse has to be withdrawn. Withdrawing attention(e.g., reprimands) does not mean the adolescent will simply be ignored for behaving any way that he chooses. He may lose the right to engage in a favorite activity or have to forego other rewards. Thus, the adolescent learns that inappropriate behavior costs (e.g., loss of privileges) rather

9

than pays (e.g., being the center of attention). Since an adolescent would not misbehave to produce particular consequences unless he viewed these consequences as desirable, perhaps many of these same consequences could be used in strengthening appropriate actions. Such may be accomplished by making the desired consequences available only for productive behaviors. For example, a student could receive recognition, praise, or special privileges following a worthwhile accomplishment or the learning of an appropriate response. Since learning new behaviors often requires considerable time and effort, adolescents should receive desired consequences as they gradually progress toward a goal. Likewise, the person controlling the consequences must remain consistent in withholding and delivering consequences if the adolescent is to learn the rules of the game.

Involve the Adolescent

Despite the efforts of adults, adolescents sometimes continue to behave in ways which adults perceive as inappropriate. The lack of progress in influencing behaviors may be the result of a failure to involve adolescents. Effective consequence management does not mean that adolescents must conform to adult standards. Adults who try to force their values on youngsters may do more harm than good. For example, consider the controversy created by trying to force adolescent submission on such trivial matters as hair style and dress. Then, too, consider the possible harm when adults singlehandedly make important decisions (e.g., determine discipline, decide what is to be studied in school) without discussing the issue with the person affected most—the adolescent. Similarly, there is no advantage in attempting to be surreptitious in influencing adolescents. An individual who is aware of what is wanted from him, who knows the payoff for appropriate behavior, the cost for inappropriate behavior, and who helps in making all these decisions is in a good position to change his behavior. The alternatives are before him, and he can make a choice.

Record Behavior Changes

Whether behavior improves or gets worse cannot be ascertained reliably through subjective evaluations. For example, one inappropriate response on the part of an adolescent may be sufficient to distort adult judgment. The inappropriate response may not even be related to the behavior being changed. Suppose an adolescent is making gradual progress on an academic task, but on a single occasion becomes irritated with a teacher request and curses or gives the "finger" to the teacher. The inappropriate social responses could conceivably taint the teacher's evaluation of the youth's academic work. Progress, therefore, needs to be recorded on a day-to-day basis for the specific behavior under consideration.

10

Graphing behavior changes is a reliable, objective method for obtaining evidence of the direction and magnitude of behavior changes. Even slight changes may be noticeable through graphing, and such feedback may provide the encouragement to keep working when subjective evaluations would have led to other decisions. Objective measurement, such as graphing, permits the adolescent to see for himself in which direction his behavior is going. Possible sources of disagreement are thus decreased. For example, the adolescent is less prone to believe that he is being indicted for poor performance simply because the teacher does not like him. Finally, objective recording of behavior indicates when the goals derived from adult and adolescent planning have been reached.

The Final Goal

The ultimate goal of all education should be effective self-management. One learns to manage his own behavior in a dependable, structured environment. A person, for instance, could not learn in a world with no certainty, no restraints. He would have no way to determine whether a behavior would lead to pleasure or disaster. Right and wrong could not be ascertained because there would be no consistent feedback from the environment. The only way an individual can learn to manage behavior, then, is from the consequences produced by his behavior. The individual who sees that certain behaviors pay and that others cost is learning self-management. He is learning to make choices to produce wanted consequences.

The role of adults in helping adolescents achieve self-management is to assist in identifying desirable behaviors, to aid in controlling the consequences for appropriate and inappropriate behavior, and to offer objective measures for evaluating progress. When adults and adolescents work cooperatively to manage consequences, the eventual absence of the adult will not diminish the adolescent's ability to manage his own behavior. When the adolescent is deprived of the opportunity of having consistent consequences follow his behavior, when others make decisions for him, or when he is forced to accept adult authority, his ability to direct his own actions will most assuredly be retarded. Proper planning and commitment, therefore, can reduce the possibility that the adolescent years will be a time of "storm and stress."

References

Bandura, A. The stormy decade: Fact or fiction? In R.E. Grinder (Ed.), Studies in adolescence: A book of readings in adolescent development. Toronto: The Macmillan Co., 1969. Pp. 16-24.

SECTION ONE

SELF-MANAGEMENT OF BEHAVIOR

Self-determination is a goal to which most of us publicly or privately aspire. We do not like to think of ourselves as pawns of fate or as objects of external manipulation. We prefer to perceive man as making decisions and determining the nature of his environmental experiences. The ultimate reality of personal volition or external determination, as the authors see it, cannot be empirically substantiated. But since it is much more reinforcing to believe in personal choice, why not help people behave in ways that would support this belief? In other words, the goal of behavior modification would be teaching people to develop internal behavior controls, to determine their own setting events, and to supply their own rewards and punishment. If such a goal could be attained, the adolescent would not be dependent on his parents, his teachers, or anyone else to provide cues and reinforcement for appropriate behavior. If the adolescent wanted to emit behavior X and stop emitting Y, he would be able to create the necessary circumstances for accomplishing these behavior changes.

All the studies included in this section provide useful information regarding the logistics of self-management. Blackwood's article describes a procedure for conditioning the adolescent to produce his own verbal controls at times of temptation. Duncan's study elucidates some of the basic procedures used in self-management, e.g., specifying the target behavior, systematically recording that behavior, and arranging consequences which would maximize the probability of desirable behavior. Broden, Hall, and Mitts' article elaborates upon one of the concepts alluded to in Duncan's article, that of self-recording the target behavior. Apparently, self-recording per se is an effective means of accomplishing behavior change. However, as Broden et al. point out, external support may be needed to sustain a change initially produced through self-recording. The possibility of adolescents controlling their own reinforcement contingencies is suggested in Glynn's article. This article indicates that one of the best ways to teach adolescents to reward themselves in a systematic, productive fashion is first to allow them to operate under externally controlled, systematic contingencies.

13

THE OPERANT CONDITIONING OF VERBALLY MEDIATED SELF-CONTROL IN THE CLASSROOM

RALPH O. BLACKWOOD

Since Ayllon & Michael's (1959) study, operant conditioning methods have been repeatedly successful in reducing the frequency of undesired behaviors in social groups (Woody, 1966). Clearly, operant techniques are welcomed additions to the skills of teachers, attendants, and other group workers. However, reduction of misbehavior does not necessarily mean elimination of misbehavior. In fact, the data often show that, while the unwanted behavior is reduced enough to be highly reinforcing to teachers, the post-treatment rate of misbehavior remains high enough to handicap educational, therapeutic, and custodial programs. For example, while Hall, Lund, & Jackson (1968) successfully increased study behavior of children who had been disruptive or had dawdled, their graphs indicated that, after treatment, the children still disrupted class or dawdled about 5 to 20% of the time. In an impressively successful study, Madsen, Becker, & Thomas (1968) found that the most successful treatment reduced disruptive classroom behaviors to 15.1%. Ward & Baker (1968), in another successful experiment, reported a reduction in disruptive behavior from 74% to 37%. Nelson (1968-69) found that out of seven primary school teachers, each of whom applied operant methods to one child, only two completely eliminated the target behavior. In each of these studies, and in most other reports of operant conditioning in social groups, misbehaviors have been strikingly reduced — but the teacher was still confronted with serious disruptive behaviors. After behavior has been modified the teacher still needs help.

The present report describes a new method which, although it builds upon traditional behavior modification, makes more comprehensive use of operant conditioning principles and their potential applications to verbal behavior. First, in a theoretical discussion the new method will be derived from operant conditioning principles. Second, a pilot experiment will be described showing how the method was developed. Third, a controlled experiment will be reported which was designed to test the effectiveness of the new method. For clarity, the theory will be stated dogmatically even though the success of the experiments does not necessarily imply that the theory is valid.

Traditionally, behavior modification has depended upon direct conditioning while the verbal behavior of children has been ignored unless the verbal behavior itself was the target. Traditional behavior modification might be called *non-mediated control*. In contrast, the new method presented here employs, in addition to traditional non-mediated control, operantly conditioned *verbally mediated control*. This verbally mediated control is based upon the assumption that, when a child is tempted to

JOURNAL OF SCHOOL PSYCHOLOGY, 1970 Vol. 8, pp. 251-258.

misbehave, he often thinks before, while, and after acting. When he thinks in words, overt or covert, the words mediate between the temptation (the stimulus situation which tends to evoke misbehavior) and the target response. Also, the child's words may mediate between a behavior and a delayed reinforcement. By applying operant techniques to these mediating words, we can achieve more precise control.

That words, or chains of words, mediate between temptation and the target behaviors, and that target behaviors can be modified by operant control of mediating verbalizations, can be derived from basic principles of operant conditioning. If principles of stimulus control are generalized to the child's verbal behavior, it follows that his own words can have stimulus control over his other behaviors. That is, certain words can act as negative discriminative stimuli, or warnings, suppressing the target responses. For example, a verbal description of the aversive consequences of a behavior can suppress that behavior if, in the past when the child initiated the target response, someone warned him of what would happen (i.e., described the consequences) and if, whenever he made the response in the presence of the warning, he suffered the aversive consequences. Under these conditions, the warning (i.e., the verbal description of the consequences of the behavior) gains stimulus control over the behavior; the child learns a discriminated avoidance response. Behavior modification is most efficient if we can condition self-control. The above analysis merely explains teacher control and how the teacher's words gain stimulus control over the child's behavior. However, due to semantic similarity, the stimulus control of the teacher's warning generalizes to the child's self-warning. This principle of stimulus generalization to semantically similar stimuli implies that *if* the child warned himself, he would cease the target response. But that "if" is too often overlooked; self-control does not develop automatically from control by others. We cannot expect the teacher's verbal control to lead to self-control unless we condition the child to produce his own verbal stimuli at the time of temptation. That is, the verbal self-warning response must be put under stimulus control of the tempting situation. It is possible, enploying the well-known methods of establishing stimulus control, to condition a chain so that when the tempting situation occurs, the child describes to himself the consequences of misbehaviors and this warning stimulus, in turn, suppresses the misbehavior. The principle of response induction suggests that this chain can be conditioned with the child's mediating verbal behavior occuring overtly but that, in the classroom, the same verbal behavior would occur covertly.

Words can act not only as warnings but also as promises (discriminative stimuli which increase the probability of a response). If, when a child is tempted to misbehave, the teacher describes the reinforcing consequences of appropriate behavior, this conditioned verbal reinforcer may increase the probability of the appropriate behavior and, if the two are mutually incompatible, it should also decrease the probability of unwanted behavior.

Words emitted by the child can mediate between temptation and the target response. They can also mediate between the target response and delayed consequences. Since delayed consequences often have little effect upon response probability and many of the important consequences of social and academic behaviors are delayed, a weak immediate reinforcement often exerts more control than a powerful delayed one of opposite valence. However, gaps in time between responses and delayed reinforcers can be "bridged" with conditioned reinforcers. A child's own verbal description of reinforcing consequences of a behavior can act as a conditioned reinforcer. Therefore, if a child is taught to describe the positive reinforcing consequences of appropriate behavior, and if this description is under stimulus control of target behavior, then whenever the behavior occurs it will be followed by the child's verbal description which acts as a conditioned reinforcer. Threfore, if a child is taught to describe the positive reinforcing consequences of appropriate behavior, and if this description is under stimulus control of target behavior, then whenever the behavior occurs it will be followed by the child's verbal description which acts as a conditioned reinforcer. In a sense, the behavior becomes self - strengthening. Similarly, if descriptions of aversive or non - reinforcing consequences are put under stimulus control of unwanted target behaviors, self-weakening of the target behaviors will occur as they are emitted and followed by conditioned aversive stimuli. So, verbal conditioned reinforcers describing important delayed consequences can cancel small immediate reinforcers.

To summarize the theoretical argument: (a) verbal behavior emitted by a child can mediate between tempting stimulus situations and target behaviors, and (b) the child's verbal behavior, as conditioned reinforcers, can cancel opposing, immediate reinforcers. To produce these effects, verbal descriptions of the consequences of target behaviors should be put under stimulus control of the tempting situations and also under stimulus control of the target behaviors so that the child will exert verbal stimulus control over himself and also will verbally reinforce his own behavior. Thus, traditional behavior modification supplemented by operantly conditioned verbal mediation should produce more precise control.

DEVELOPING A METHOD FOR VERBAL MEDIATION TRAINING

The procedures for training children to think of the consequences of their behaviors were developed in the following exploratory study. Twenty-five eighth and ninth graders were selected as subjects for a traditional behavior modification study. The teacher selected the five children who most frequently disrupted each of his classes. The new contingencies of reinforcement were effective, reducing the frequency of the target behaviors by 49%. However, learning activities continued to be interrupted frequently. In fact, disruptive behaviors were still emitted, although at a decreased rate, by 13 of the 25 children. The frequency of misbehaviors of the other children had decreased to zero.

In an attempt to discover other reinforcing contingencies which might explain the differences in reactions to operant techniques, the 25 children were interviewed individually. Several children who had not previously exhibited behavior problems were also interviewed. The interviews were initiated with nondirective probes and open-ended questions, and proceeded to direct questions. It soon became apparent that most of the self-controlled children verbalized the consequences of both disruptive and acceptable behaviors. Also, their verbalizations included descriptions of both immediate and delayed consequences, descriptions which were rich in imagery. They often discussed the relative merits of small immediate rewards versus more powerful delayed consequences. In contrast, not one of the 12 misbehaving children fluently verbalized the consequences of his behaviors; when asked direct questions, the misbehaving children produced only sketchy and inaccurate verbal pictures of delayed rewards and punishments.

To test the hypothesis that fluent

verbalization of the reinforcement contingencies is related to self-control, the originally planned study was interrupted and a pilot study was conducted using one misbehaving child. This child had left his' seat without permission an average of 6.3 times each class period. Traditional operant techniques had reduced this to an average of 4.5 times each period. To establish verbal mediating chains, the child was given a typed paragraph which described his misbehavior and its aversive consequences to him as well as the desired behaviors and their reinforcing consequences. He was assigned practice which was designed to condition the descriptions as strong verbal response chains and put them under stimulus control of the tempting situations. Exercises included copying the essay, paraphrasing it, writing it in his own words from memory, reciting it orally from memory, and role playing (that is, acting out the target behavior and alternative behaviors while verbalizing the consequences aloud). The mediation training might be described as escape-avoidance learning. The child was kept after school and assigned a certain amount of work (e.g., making one copy of the essay). When he finished the assigned task, he was allowed to go home; but when he refused to cooperate, the assignment was increased and he was detained longer.

After considerable trial-and-error exploration during which the paragraph was rewitten to make it more concrete and more meaningful to the child, the misbehavior decreased rapidly in frequency and, during the role playing phase, entirely ceased to occur.

While an uncontrolled study involving only one subject does not provide confirming evidence, it was useful in developing the operant mediation method. To test the hypothesis that operant verbal mediation training reduces the misbehaviors of children who, after receiving traditional behavior modification treatment continue to misbehave, a controlled study was carried out.

METHOD

Subjects. The subjects were 12 eighth and ninth grade children (11 boys and one girl) who continued to emit disruptive behaviors after eight weeks of traditional behavior modification treatment. These were the children who were interviewed in the pilot study described earlier. They ranged from 14 to 16 years of age; three had repeated a grade.

Design. The design was a Pretest-Posttest Control Group Design (Campbell & Stanley, 1963) with the 12 children randomly separated into an experimental and a control group. There were one to three target children in each of the teacher's classes. During the treatment period, copying, paraphrasing, and oral recitation of the essays were used as punishment for any target misbehavior. Experimental subjects were administered mediation essays; control subjects were given an essay which did not discuss the consequences of misbehavior.

Daily observations were made by the classroom teacher, who observed the class during lecture, discussion, and recitation, and recorded each target response and the time of its occurrence. Observations were made during the first 30 minutes of the 50 minute period. Then the teacher assigned the children written work at their seats and, while the children worked, the teacher continued to observe and reviewed in memory the previous 30 minute observation period, correcting any recordings which were incomplete due to the problem of recording and teaching simultaneously. For five days during the baseline period and five days during the post-treatment period, another teacher visited the classroom and observed the 12 children from the back of the room. Observations were collected for 10 school days prior to the initiation of treatment and post-treatment observations were collected for 15 school days after termination of treatment on each child.

Materials. Two types of essays were constructed: mediation essays to be administered to the experimental group and a punishment essay to be administered to the control group. Five different mediation essays were prepared, one for each class of target behaviors. Each mediation essay contained four questions and their answers. First was the question, "What did I' do wrong?" and a sentence describing the target behavior of the child for whom the essay was designed, e.g., "I was talking without permission." A second question asked why the target behavior was inappropriate. For example, "Why should I not blurt out whatever comes into my head?" This second question was followed by a paragraph describing vividly and in the children's vocabulary the aversive consequences of the undesirable behavior: e.g., "If I disrupt the class by talking without permission, I may have to stay after school or write this essay. Also, while talking I may miss important things. Then I will not be able to understand what the class is doing and class will be dull and boring. Time will drag slowly for me while others will find the assignments interesting." The third question asked what the child should have been doing; it was followed by a brief but concrete description of the desired behavior: e.g., "I should raise my hand when I wish to speak, keeping my mouth closed until the teacher signals that I may talk." The fourth and last question asked the reasons for the desired behaviors. For example, "Why should I get permission before speaking?" It was followed by a concrete description of the reinforcing consequences of the desired behaviors. The descriptions of consequences also contained references to the tempting situations: e.g., "Even if I have a very interesting idea, I should get permission before speaking. Then the teacher and my classmates will be more likely to listen to what I have to say." The essays were mimeographed, single-spaced, and occupied less than one page.

The punishment essay administered to the control group was of approximately the same length, reading level, and style as the mediation essays. However, it described the working of a steam engine.

PROCEDURE

The following plan was explained to the children the day before treatment was initiated. If a child misbehaved, a copy of an essay would be dropped on his desk. This was a sign that the student owed the teacher two handwritten copies of the essay. However, if he did not complain or ask questions when given the essay and if he engaged in no additional misbehaviors during the remainder of the period, then he could petition, after class, for a reduction of the assignment to only one copy.

If the assigned work was not submitted the next day, the assignment would be doubled. If the doubled assignment was not submitted when due, the child would be given a detention slip which he had to take home and have signed by his parent or guardian. If the child failed to stay for detention, this punishment would be increased to two days' detention. A second failure to comply would result in the child's being sent to the Principal's office with a recommendation for severe treatment. The plan was explained in detail, but it was not expected that the explanation would have much, if any, stimulus control over the 12 children serving as subjects.

Most of the 12 children misbehaved and were assigned essays during the next two days. When the essay was dropped on the student's desk, the typical response was, "What'd I get this for? I ain't done nothin!" However, the teacher simply continued the lesson and ignored such remarks. When a child accepted his essay without comment, the teacher smiled and made an approving remark designed to enhance his status with his peers and indicated that the child should stop by after class to get his assignment reduced to one copy of the essay.

Students were instructed to submit essays upon entering the class. When an essay was handed to him, the teacher smiled, complimented the student, and made comments to enhance his status among his peers. If a child failed to submit his essay, he was completely ignored until seat work had been assigned and the children were concentrating on their assignments. Then the teacher approached him and dealt with the case quietly, briefly, and firmly but with no arguing. Usually a child was also reminded that failure to bring the doubled assignment the next day would lead to detention. It was suggested that the easiest and smartest solution was to copy the essays, hand them in, and forget the idea of "beating the game," because non-cooperation would inevitably lead to greater punishment.

. A child who stayed for detention had to be motivated to participate in the mediation training and yet positive reinforcers could not be used without rewarding the misbehaviors which led to detention. This had become evident when, during some earlier attempts to control behaviors, children kept after school were allowed to erase boards, line up chairs, arrange science equipment, and take part in discussions in which the teacher was non-directive and reflected feelings. These positively reinforcing activities, when made contingent upon being assigned detention, had increased the frequency of misbehaviors. So it seemed inadvisable to use positive reinforcers to motivate children and yet, when given such an assignment, a child can loaf and later

report to his friends that he has won points by refusing to do assigned work. The solution seemed to be escape-avoidance conditioning; detention was made highly aversive and cooperation was rewarded with release from detention. The teacher announced that when a satisfactory amount of work of good quality was completed, a child would be allowed to go. In spite of the announcement, a number of children stubbornly refused to cooperate, making such statements as "You ain't gonna make me write nothin." These remarks were ignored. The most cooperative child was released early, perhaps after 20 minutes of detention. In the beginning, release from detention was made contingent upon cooperation rather than upon amount or quality of work. This soon produced cooperative behaviors in the others. On the first day five boys were on detention and four refused to do anything. After 20 minutes the one boy who cooperated was released and the others were told that, by cooperating, they could just as easily leave before the hour was over. One after the other began writing until only one boy had to stay until the end of the hour. From that day on, there was usually a high level of cooperation during the detention period, although the children repeatedly begged to be allowed to erase boards, clean equipment, pick up papers, or anything other than write the essays.

The mediation training was administered in several stages. The first two times a child misbehaved, he was assigned an essay to copy and could do his work at home. The purpose of this task was simply to familiarize the children with the content and to develop habits of cooperation. On the third misbehavior, the child was kept after school and directed to paraphrase the essay. If the child continued to misbehave, he was assigned the paraphrasing task for four consecutive misbehaviors. Paraphrasing was expected to produce descriptions of reinforcement contingencies which would be more meaningful to the child. After paraphrasing the essay four times, on the eighth, ninth, and tenth misbehaviors the child was kept after school and required to write the essay in his own words from memory. If he had difficulty recalling the ideas, the teacher provided prompts or probes. The final state of treatment, for children who continued to misbehave, was for the child to sit in his regular seat and orally describe both the situation which typically stimulated his misbehavior and also how he would think when again tempted. Sometimes he was directed to act out the misbehavior and the desired behavior and to describe the consequences. The latter two stages of training were designed to strengthen the response chains, put them under stimulus control of the tempting situations, and also put them under stimulus control of the target behaviors.

RESULTS

Reliability of observations was checked by comparing observations of the teacher and the visiting observer. To be counted as an agreement, observers had to agree both on the occurrence of a behavior and on the time at which it occurred. The teacher and the visiting observers agreed on the frequency of the target responses for 86% of the class periods during the pre-treatment period. The post-treatment observations were in agreement 98% of the time. High inter-observer reliability may be attributable to (a) the choice of easily observed behaviors, (b) recording only one response class for each child, and (c) the high frequency, during the posttreatment observation period, of class periods with zero responses.

The frequency of the target behavior of five of the mediation-trained children decreased to zero and remained at that level throughout the 15-day post-treatment observation period. Of the five, misbehavior ended for one child after copying the essay twice, for two children after paraphrasing the essay, for one during oral recitation, and only two children were given the role playing treatment. The sixth mediation-trained child continued his misbehavior but at a lower frequency than previously (0.6 responses per day versus the earlier 4.9 responses per day). The responses of all but one child in the control group also decreased. However, only one control child's misbehavior was completely eliminated. Table 1 presents for each child the types of misbehavior and the mean number of misbehaviors at each observation phase: before the traditional training, after traditional training, and after the controlled study.

The mean reduction in number of misbehaviors for the mediation trained group during the controlled experiment was 3.1 responses per day as contrasted with 0.4 for the punished group. To ascertain if the improvement of the experimental group was significantly greater than that of the control group, a Mann-Whitney U Test was performed on the difference scores. The difference was significant ($U=1$; $P=.004$), indicating that mediation training was more effective than the punishment procedures in further reducing misbehaviors after traditional behavior modification methods had been employed. Also, the Mann-Whitney U Test indicated that the mediation trained group made significant gains ($U=0$; $P=.002$) but that the punished group gains were not significant ($U=15$; $P=.70$). At the end of the experiment, the mean number of misbehaviors per day for the mediation trained subjects was 0.1, as contrasted to a mean of 2.5 for the punished subjects. This difference in posttreatment frequency of misbehavior of the two groups was significant, as determined by the Mann-Whitney U Test ($U=1$; $P=.004$).

Table 1
Type of Misbehavior and Mean Frequency of Misbehavior During Baseline Period, During Observations After Traditional Behavior Modification, And During Observations After Mediation Training

Subject Number	Type of Misbehavior	Mean Frequency of Misbehavior per Class Period		
		Baseline	After Traditional Methods	After Mediation Methods
Mediation Trained Subjects				
1	Blurting out	5.5	0.9	0.0
2	Talking to neighbors	7.0	2.2	0.0
3	Hitting neighbors	5.8	3.6	0.0
4	Distracting noises	6.4	3.6	0.0
5	Blurting out	5.8	3.8	0.0
6	Out of seat	6.5	4.9	0.6
Subjects Given Punishment Essay				
7	Distracting noises	5.9	0.7	0.0
8	Talking to neighbors	5.3	1.9	0.9
9	Out of seat	5.5	2.9	2.8
10	Out of seat	6.4	2.9	3.3
11	Insolent remarks	6.8	3.6	3.0
12	Blurting out	6.6	5.2	4.8
Means				
Mediation Group Means		6.2	3.2	0.1
Punishment Group Means		6.1	2.9	2.5
Grand Means		6.1	3.0	2.6

DISCUSSION AND CONCLUSIONS

Although caution should be employed in drawing conclusions from a preliminary study in which (a) the teacher is also an experimenter, (b) post-treatment observations cover only 15 days, and (c) there is no replication as far as teacher effects are concerned, the controlled experiment reported here indicates that traditional behavior modification methods can be improved by adding mediation training and that mediation training is more effective, following traditional behavior modificaton, than is mere punishment.

REFERENCES

AYLLON, T., & MICHAEL, J. The psychiatric nurse as a behavioral engineer. *Journal of the Experimental Analysis of Behavior,* 1959, *2,* 323-334.

CAMPBELL, D. T., & STANLEY, J. C. Experimental and quasi-experimental designs for research in teaching. In N. L. Gage (Ed.), *Handbook of research on teaching.* Chicago: Rand McNally, 1963. Pp. 171-246.

HALL, R. V., LUND, D., & JACKSON, D. Effects of teacher attention on study behavior. *Journal of Applied Behavior Analysis,* 1968, *1,* 1-12.

MADSEN, C. H., JR., BECKER, W. C., & THOMAS, D. R. Rules, praise, and ignoring: Elements of elementary classroom control. *Journal of Applied Behavior Analysis,* 1968, *1,* 139-150.

NELSON, W. H. Teachers as experimenters. *Journal of School Psychology,* 1968-69, *3,* 29-34.

WARD, M. H., & BAKER, B. L. Reinforcement therapy in the classroom. *Journal of Applied Behavior Analysis,* 1968, *1,* 323-328.

WOODY, R. H. Behavior therapy and school psychology. *Journal of School Psychology,* 1966, *4,* 1-4.

SELF-APPLICATION OF BEHAVIOR MODIFICATION TECHNIQUES BY TEEN-AGERS[1] [2]

Ann Dell Duncan, Ph.D.[3] [4]

Would you like to lose weight? Stop swearing and being sarcastic? Have beautiful fingernails? Teen-agers reported in this study wanted to, and did. They found by applying precise behavior management techniques to specific problems they could experience that elusive phenomenon called self-control.

Definitions of self-control vary with the researcher. For Kanfer (1966), self-control is the behavior which occurs in the presence of conflicting response tendencies. Goldiamond (1965) prefers to discuss the functional relationship between the individual's behavior and the environment. Ferster *et al.* (1962) refers to self-control as "some specific performances which will lower the disposition to emit the behavior to be controlled (p. 88)."

The elusiveness of self-control may be in the lack of a precise definition. For the moralists among us, self-control is when one does what is right. For the psychodynamically oriented, it is achieved by controlling the inner-forces and redirecting them towards more constructive patterns. For this researcher, self-control is *procedurally* defined as the self-selection and application of behavior modification techniques.

Teachers (Lindsley, 1966), parents of children with retarded behaviors (Sebastian, 1967), and a community agency (Holzschuh, 1968) have successfully applied precise behavior management techniques. These adults were given brief instructions in behavior analysis and sent out to record one or more behaviors (Lindsley, 1967a). Teen-agers in this study learned to analyze their selected behavior targets by recording and plotting daily rates of occurrence. They precisely measured the effects of altering their environments with contingent consequences.

ADOLESCENCE, 1969, Vol. 4, pp. 541-556.

METHOD

Participants

Fifty-five high school seniors (enrolled in a psychology class at a suburban high school) volunteered to participate in this project. Their previous exposure to behavior modification consisted of reading ten pages of an introductory psychology text section about Skinner and pigeon operant conditioning. The median age was 17. There were 38 girls and 17 boys. These were not deviant young adults, just normal teen-agers finishing up the last semester of their high school careers.

Procedures

The psychology instructor asked the volunteers to sign up for one of three meeting nights. The author met with two groups; one at the high school, the other at the medical center. The third group met with another graduate student at his apartment. Each group met for approximately two hours once a week for eight weeks. They presented their projects to the other group members. There were no "formal" lectures.

The teen-agers learned behavior modification in three steps: pinpointing their behavior targets; recording and plotting the rate of occurrence daily; and altering the environment. The target behaviors were self-selected, the movement rates self-recorded, and alterations self-selected and self-applied. Contingencies were set for attendance at every group meeting. For example, in order to come to the second meeting, each student was required to record six days of data.

Equipment

The only equipment provided was tally sheets and six-cycle semi-logarithmic graph paper which has been standardized to facilitate across behavior comparisons (Lindsley, 1967a). Three alternative types of counters were suggested: the Domatic Wrist Counter (Lindsley, 1968), a less expensive plastic golf-score caddy, or a knitting-stitch counter which fits over the end of a pencil. The majority of the students used the plastic golf-score caddy, which may be purchased from local sporting goods stores for about

85 cents.

RESULTS

Thirty-three of the 55 enrolled turned in reports of successful behavior modification projects. Ninety-thee percent of the 33 projects were deceleration targets. The six projects selected for detailed presentation include one each of the four most common deceleration targets. Figure 1 summarizes the median emission rates of the deceleration targets before modification. (See all Figures at end of article). The ranges of these phase-one medians and the median of that distribution are reported. It is interesting to note that with an eqqual number of projects, nail biting rates range over four log-cycles (from five per day to one per minute), whereas face touching only covers one-half of one log-cycle (from four to eight times every 100 minutes).

Food Reaches

Teen-age girls select losing weight as a target behavior more frequently than boys. Ferster's (1962) obese woman attempted to decelerate their weight and caloric intake. If decelerating weight on the body is the target, then the measure should not be the bathroom scale. Rather, the more precise measure would be the behavior which puts pounds on in the first place—that is, food reaches, snacks, or chews per minute.

Debbie recorded her rate of eating snacks between meals (Figure 2). During phase one, her median snack rate was .007 per minute. In other words, she ate seven snacks during 16½ hours. After it was mutually agreed by Debbie and her group members that she had sufficiently stable premodification data, the group suggested alternative decelerating consequences. Since it was close to Senior Prom time, Debbie wanted to lose weight and decelerate her snacks fairly rapidly.

From the suggested alternatives, she chose to shock herself after every snack. She located a "joke" cigarette pack containing a small battery and coil. When the top is removed, the metal binding on the case completes the circuit and shock is administered. She required herself to hold the shock pack for ten seconds. At the next meeting when she presented her graphed data, it was evident that the shock after she ate the food significantly decelerated snack-

24

ing between meals to a median of five per day.

She then tried shocking herself as she reached for food. In the presence of food, every time she reached she self-applied ten seconds of shock. The between-meals food-reaching decelerated to only once per day. This resulted in such a weight loss that she was able to fit into the formal she wanted to wear to the prom. The significant differences in snacking were computed using the Lindsley Mid-Median test (1967b), based on Fisher's Exact Probability Test (Siegel, 1956). The exact probability level of the difference between phase one and three was $p = .00,02$.

Swearing

Dave said at the first meeting that what he really wanted to get rid of was all his swearing. Swearing embarrassed him, especially on dates. Dave counted his swearing rate on the Domatic wrist counter. He tried using the smaller, plastic golf-score caddy but his rate was so high that he could not operate the smaller counter as fast as he swore during an outburst. He recorded all day long.

His median rate during the pre-modification phase was .4 per minute or four swear words every ten minutes. Dave selected the consequence of placing a surgical gauze mask over his face, wearing it for three minutes, and not allowing himself to talk to anyone while wearing it. He immediately placed the mask over his mouth every time he swore regardless of where he was. After the first week of phase two, Dave reported he masked himself twice at a local student "hangout," once on a date, and once at home. As indicated in Figure 3, the rate markedly decelerated. Using the Lindsley Mid-Median test, this difference was highly significant ($p = .00,000,000,000,1$).

Face Touching

Of the completed behavior modification projects currently on file (total of 2,000), we find that about one out of 20 behaviors decelerates simply by recording its frequency (Lindsley, 1967a). This may be an example of a multiple-function event. The self-recording may serve both as a decelerating stimulus and a decelerating consequence. Betty decided she was simply going to record the behavior after collecting six days of pre-modification data, and noted the rate was going down. The first large rate deceleration

25

occured on the day of the second group meeting (Figure 4).

Nail Biting

Emma reported she had bitten her nails ever since she was two years old. She recorded 11 days of pre-modification rates which indicated she bit or picked at her nails a little over once every minute of her waking day (median rate). With some assistance from her group members, she selected wearing gloves as her consequence. For every bite or pick she wore a glove on the nail-bitten hand for five minutes (Figure 5).

For the first five days of phase two, she wore a pair of winter gloves. At the end of the fifth day when Emma got home from school, her mother presented her with a pair of huge, flaming red mittens which she had made. Emma did not bite or pick her nails for three days. After seventeen days of the contingency-consequence of red mittens, Emma went on a weekend trip with the high school band. She left her mittens at home but took her counter. Nail biting and picking immediately accelerated, although not to the former rate. She then reapplied the contingency and the rate again decelerated. Changes in the behavior were highly significant across phases one through four ($p = .00,000,000,01$).

Knuckle Cracking

Patty cracked her knuckles at a median rate of once every five minutes. She stated it was interfering with her dating but she wasn't sure of what kind of consequence to select. Her little brother suggested she wear his "monster hand" every time she crackled her knuckles. However, she had another set of knuckles needing a consequence. Her little brother offered to loan her one of his much prized boxing gloves. Patty wore the glove and the "hand" and her knuckle cracking rate dropped to .03 per minute or once every thirty-five minutes (Figure 6). After three days she withdrew the contingency and consequence, whereupon the behavior decelerated even further. This was an excellent example of an event which could decelerate upon presentation as well as upon removal: a double-barreled variable. The differences across phases was highly significant (phase one-three $p = .00,000,009$).

Sarcasms

Bev defined sarcasms as any put-down comment which may

or may not hurt someone. She had a list of the ones commonly in her repertoire and added to it as she became more skillful in the assessment of her own behavior. Two days after starting the project, she was in a minor automobile accident which decelerated the behavior but did not eliminate it. For phase one, she was sarcastic a median rate of three times every two hours. Bev decided to apply a surgical gauze mask after every sarcastic remark and keep it on for five minutes. Sarcasms decreased to four a day (Figure 7). The Senior Prom was the next weekend and she did not want to take the mask with her to the dance. She removed the contingency for the weekend and the behavior did not accelerate (both she and her boy friend counted over the weekend). She reapplied the contingent mask-wearing and the behavior decelerated even further. The exact probability level between phase one and four was p = . 00,000,000,7.

DISCUSSION

Teen-agers can control their own behavior by self-applying behavior modification techniques. Given minimal instructions, a tally sheet, graph paper, and some assistance in pinpointing target behaviors, they can effectively and efficiently change behaviors their parents had complained about for years. One mother said that she hadn't seen her daughter so happy since before junior high school. The girl had never lost her "baby fat" but had continually gained weight instead. When she recorded her food-reaching rate, applied a decelerating consequence, and lost weight, her social world brightened up. Now the mother and daughter plot food-reach records and keep an eye on each other's graphs, which are posted on the refrigerator door.

One concern before this project started was the self-recording. Other disciplines, such as psychiatry and social psychology, frequently accept self-report as valid and reliable. We wanted to determine the validity of their self-rate records and thus had their classmates certify the project while in progress. Teen-agers were randomly assigned to each other and counted the same behavior as the self-recorder for several samples during the study. In all instances, the information collected by both recorders agreed within a frequency of 1 or 2.

A randomly selected number of projects were followed up. For example, six months later Dave had started to swear again but this time only in the fraternity house. For others, the target behaviors remained decelerated. Possibly the natural consequences in the environment took over and helped maintain the change brought about by synthetic programming.

Thus, teen-agers can select behaviors they wish to decelerate or accelerate, maintain rate-recording over an extended period of time, and effectively alter their environment and behavior with contingent consequences.

Skinner (1959) states, "A science of man supplies striking support for the working faith that men can build a better world, and through it, better men." It also seems likely that better men could build a better world.

FOOTNOTES

1. This project was supported in part by the National Institute of Neurological Disease and Blindness (NB -05362-05), and the National Institute of Child Health and Human Development (HD-00870-05) to the Bureau of Child Research, University of Kansas while the author was a doctoral fellow at the University of Kansas Medical Center.

2. Appreciation is extended to the Administration and faculty of Shawnee Mission North High School and especially to Mr. David Roberts, psychology instructor, who initiated this project. Charlie Galloway led one of the groups and gave willingly of his time and efforts to make this project a success. To the young adults whose enthusiasm and interest were the sparks of this project, go my deepest appreciation, for without their behavior this study would not have been possible.

3. To Dr. Ogden R. Lindsley, mentor extraordinary, go my thanks for stimulating me towards this research boulevard and for his perceptive assistance in all phases of this project.

4. Now at the Ferkauf Graduate School, Department of Special Education, Yeshiva University, New York City, New York.

PHASE ONE, BEHAVIOR RATES

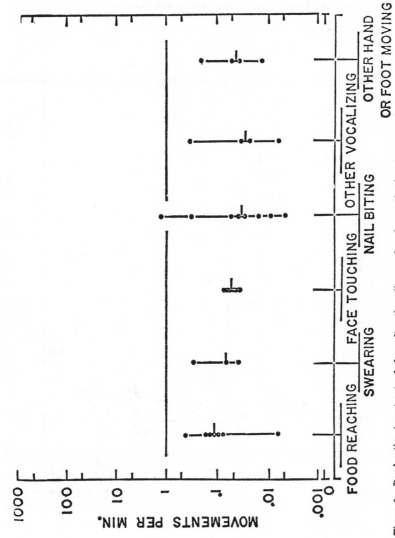

Figure 1. Deceleration target rates before alteration all occur less frequently than two per minute.

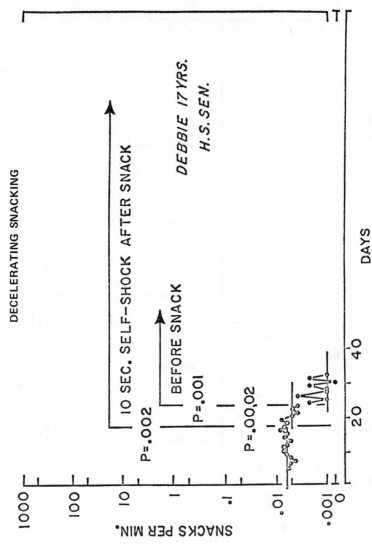

DECELERATING SNACKING

Figure 2. Self-application of shock after (consequence) each snack decelerated snacking between meals. Then self-application of shock before (stimulus) each snack further decelerated snacking.

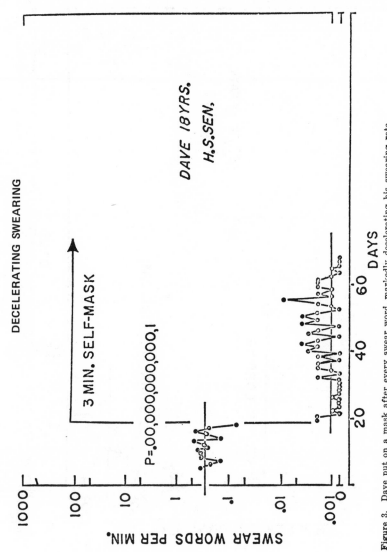

Figure 3. Dave put on a mask after every swear word, markedly decelerating his swearing rate.

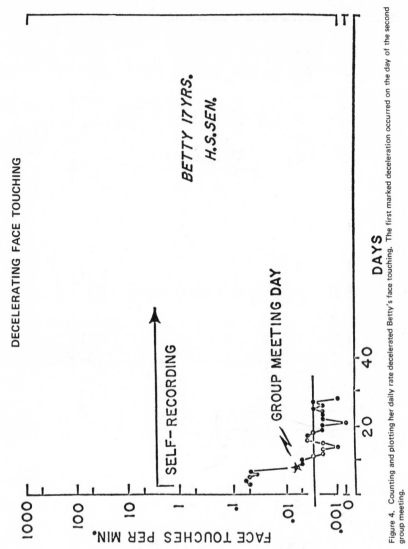

DECELERATING FACE TOUCHING

FACE TOUCHES PER MIN.

DAYS

SELF–RECORDING

GROUP MEETING DAY

BETTY 17 YRS.
H.S. SEN.

Figure 4. Counting and plotting her daily rate decelerated Betty's face touching. The first marked deceleration occurred on the day of the second group meeting.

32

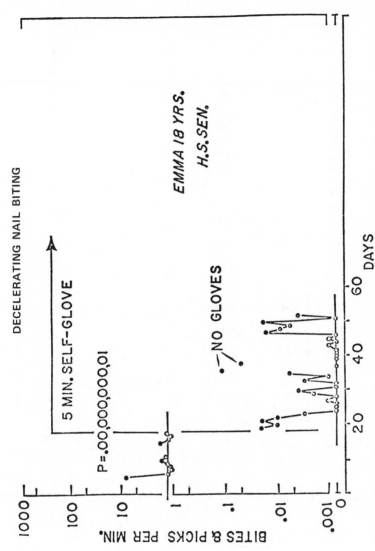

Figure 5. Effect of contingent self-application of gloves decelerated nail biting and picking. Note the faster rate of biting and picking during the two days without the glove contingency.

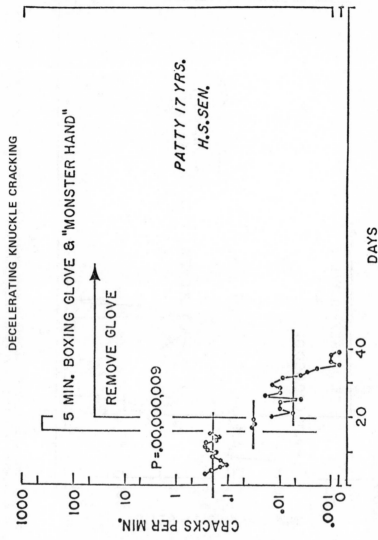

Figure 6. This consequence decelerated knuckle cracking when presented and when withdrawn.

34

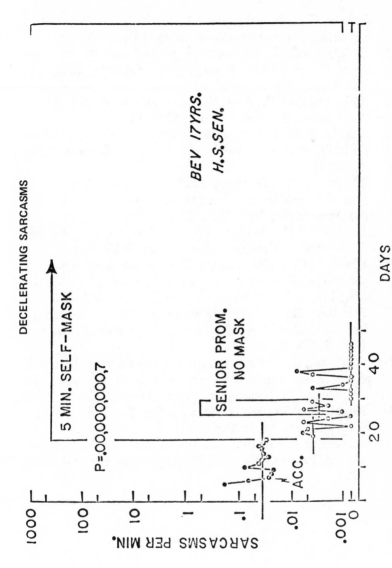

Figure 7. Self-masking decelerated sarcastic comments. No increase in rate occurred during the Senior Prom when this procedure was temporarily suspended.

35

REFERENCES

1. Ferster, C.B., Nurnberger, J.I., Levitt, E.B. The control of eating. *Journal of Mathematics,* 1962, *1,* 87-109.
2. Goldiamond, I. Self-control procedures in personal behavior problems. *Psychological Reports,* 1965, *17,* 851-868.
3. Holzschuh, R.D. Annual report of the Big Brothers Association of Greater Kansas City, 1968.
4. Kanfer, F. H. Influence of age and incentive conditions on children's self-rewards. *Psychological Reports,* 1966, *19,* 263-274.
5. Lindsley, O.R. Teaching teachers to teach. Paper presented at the annual meeting of American Psychological Association, New York City, 1966.
6. Lindsley, O.R. Lecture presented to Education 115, University of Kansas, Fall semester, 1967. (a)
7. Lindsley, O.R. The mid-median test for assigning exact probabilities to precision teaching products. Unpublished manuscript, University of Kansas, 1967. (b)
8. Linsdley, O.R. A reliable wrist counter for recording behavior rates. *Journal of Applied Behavorial Analysis,* 1968, *1,* 77-78.
9. Sebastian, E. Fathers groups for behavior modification of retarded children. Paper presented at *American Association of Mental Deficiency,* Denver, Colo., 1967.
10. Siegel, S. *Nonparametric statistics for the behavior sciences,* New York: McGraw-Hill, 1956.
11. Skinner, B.F. Freedom and the control of men. In *Cumulative Record.* New York: Appleton-Century-Crofts, 1959.

THE EFFECT OF SELF-RECORDING
ON THE CLASSROOM BEHAVIOR
OF TWO EIGHTH-GRADE STUDENTS[1]

Marcia Broden, R. Vance Hall, and Brenda Mitts

Helping a student acquire appropriate study behaviors has probably been a problem since schools began. Various techniques, including counseling, special classes, and use of the leather strap have been tried. Very often these approaches have been ineffective and parents, teachers, and students have resigned themselves to a year of problems and frustration.

Since the 1960s, a concerted effort has been exerted to apply systematically behavior modification principles in the public school classroom. A number of studies have shown that giving attention for a behavior immediately after it occurred caused this behavior to increase in strength, while consistently ignoring a behavior frequently resulted in a decrease in strength. Hall and Broden (1968), Hall, Lund, and Jackson (1968), and Thomas,

Becker, and Armstrong (1968) successfully used this technique to affect study behavior in the classroom by having teachers attend only to study or non-disruptive behaviors while ignoring non-study or disruptive ones. Hall, Fox, Willard, Goldsmith, Emerson, Owen, Davis, and Porcia (1970) used teacher attention, feedback, praise, and other available reinforcers to control disputing and talking-out behaviors in various classrooms.

The use of behavior modification principles was expanded to include varied techniques by other experimenters. Madsen, Becker, and Thomas (1968) assessed the effect of rules as well as ignoring and praising behaviors. Peer control of arithmetic and spelling scores was demonstrated in a study by Evans and Oswalt (1968). Barrish, Saunders, and Wolf (1968) used a loss of classroom privileges to reduce out-of-seat and talking-out behaviors in a fourth grade class. Hall, Panyan, Rabon, and Broden (1968) showed that teacher attention, a study game, and loss of time for a between-period break were effective in increasing an entire classes' study behavior.

McKenzie, Clark, Wolf, Kothera, and Benson (1968) used a token system backed by privileges and allowances to increase academic performance in a special education classroom. Broden, Hall, Dunlap, and Clark (1970) increased study behavior in a junior

[1]The authors wish to express appreciation to observer Betty Smith and to Kenneth Tewell, Robert Clark, Larry Odom, and Leo Richter of the Bonner Springs, Kansas Public Schools for their complete cooperation in making this study possible. This study is part of the research conducted at the Juniper Gardens Children's Project and is partially supported by the National Institute of Child Health and Human Development (HD-03144-03) Bureau of Child Research and Department of Human Development and Family Life, University of Kansas.

JOURNAL OF APPLIED BEHAVIOR ANALYSIS, 1971, Vol. 4, pp. 191-199.

high special education class using a point system in which points were redeemable for privileges available in the class and school. They demonstrated that while praise was effective in modifying behaviors, praise coupled with points issued contingently for acceptable behaviors seemed more effective at the junior high level.

Each of the methods listed, while successful, involved a relatively systematic effort on the part of the teacher to initiate the behavior change or to monitor and reinforce the desired behaviors. None of these studies dealt with the problem of what to do with a student in a room where the teacher does not want to or "cannot" work with a specific student. Such situations are often found in secondary level classrooms where teacher lectures are a primary form of instruction.

The method used in the present study was self-recording. It was initially an effort to assess whether a subject's recording of his own behavior would help increase or decrease its occurrence, and whether someone not in the classroom could modify classroom behavior. It was also an attempt to assess a procedure whereby self-recording could be withdrawn with no significant decrease in study once higher study rates had been established.

EXPERIMENT I

Subject and Setting

Liza was an eighth-grade girl enrolled in a history class at Bonner Springs Junior High, Bonner Springs, Kansas. She was doing poorly in history (her grade was a D−) and had told the counselor she was interested in doing better in school. The counselor set up weekly counseling sessions with Liza but found that according to the teacher and to Liza, just talking over a problem had not carried over into the class setting.

Liza's history class met daily immediately after lunch for 40 min. The teacher, a young man, stood near the front of the room throughout most of the period. Liza sat toward the back of the room. Classes were primarily lecture sessions in which the teacher talked as he stood in the front of the class. There was some class discussion when the teacher interspersed questions within the lecture.

The counselor and the experimenter had approached the teacher about giving increased attention to Liza for study. The teacher expressed a willingness to cooperate but felt that due to the lecture format of the class and the amount of material he had to cover each day he could not consistently attend to Liza for studying. For this reason it was decided to use self-recording with the counselor as the agent for initiating and carrying out the experimental procedures.

Observation

An observer entered the classroom during a 5-min break before the class and took a seat at the back of the room. She observed for 30 min of the 40-min session, beginning when the bell rang to signify the start of class. She left during a break at the end of the class session. Pupil behaviors were recorded at the end of each 10 sec of observation. Teacher attention to Liza was recorded whenever it occurred. Liza was not told that she was being observed.

Pupil behaviors were dichotomized into study and non-study behaviors. "Study" was defined as attending to a teacher-assigned task and meant that when it was appropriate, Liza should be facing the teacher, writing down lecture notes, facing a child who was responding to a teacher question, or reciting when called upon by the teacher. "Non-study" behaviors meant that Liza was out of her seat without permission, talking out without being recognized by the teacher, facing the window, fingering non-academic objects such as her makeup, comb, purse, or working on an assignment for another class.

Data were recorded on sheets composed of double rows of squares with each square representing the passage of 10 sec of time. (See Hall, et al., 1968). The top row was used to record teacher attention which was recorded whenever the teacher called on or spoke to Liza. The bottom row was used to record Liza's study or non-study behaviors.

Reliability checks were made at least once during each phase of the study. During these checks, another observer made simultaneous and independent observations. After the observation the sheets were compared and scored interval by interval for the number of intervals of agreement. The total number of intervals of agreement were divided by the total number of intervals observed and this figure was multiplied by 100 to obtain a percentage figure. Agreement of the records for this study ranged from 87 to 96% for study behavior and 100% for teacher attention.

METHOD

Baseline

Baseline data were recorded for seven days before experimental procedures began. The counselor saw the subject twice during this time for a weekly conference (a procedure followed before recording data and continued throughout the study).

Self-Recording₁

On the eighth day of observation, the counselor met the subject in conference and gave her a slip containing three rows of 10 squares (See Fig. 1) and directed her to record her study behavior "when she thought of it" during her history class sessions. Some aspects of study behavior were discussed at this time, including a definition of what constituted studying.

Liza was instructed to take the slip to class each day and to record a "+" in the square if she was studying or had been doing so for the last few minutes, and a "−" if she was not

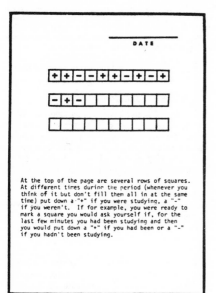

At the top of the page are several rows of squares. At different times during the period (whenever you think of it but don't fill them all in at the same time) put down a "+" if you were studying, a "−" if you weren't. If for example, you were ready to mark a square you would ask yourself if, for the last few minutes you had been studying and then you would put down a "+" if you had been or a "−" if you hadn't been studying.

Fig. 1. Sample of self-recording sheet used by Liza.

studying at the time she thought to record. Sometime before the end of the school day she was to turn it in to the counselor. The slips were available each day from the counselor and could be obtained during breaks between classes. At the weekly pupil-counselor conference, the self-recording slips were discussed and the counselor praised Liza's reports of study behavior emphasizing the days when the per cent of plus marks was high.

Baseline₂

Slips were not issued for five days (Days 14 through 18). When, on the second day of Baseline₂ Liza requested one, the counselor stated that she was out of slips and would tell her when she got more.

Self-Recording₂

Slips were once again handed to the subject by the counselor at some time before history period and Liza was instructed to record her study and non-study behavior.

Selp-Recording Plus Praise

The teacher was asked to attend to Liza "whenever he could" and to praise her for study whenever possible. Slips for self-recording continued to be available to Liza and counselor praise continued to be issued for plus marks on the self-recording slips during the weekly conference.

Praise Only

No slips were issued to Liza. Teacher attention continued at a higher rate than during Baseline.

Baseline₃

Increased teacher attention was withdrawn.

RESULTS

Baseline

Figure 2 presents a record of Liza's study behavior and of teacher verbal attention. During baseline conditions, Liza had a low rate of study (30%) despite two conferences with the counselor and promises to "really try". The mean rate of teacher attention was two times per session.

Self-Recording₁

During the Self-Recording₁ phase, when Liza began to record her classroom behavior,

39

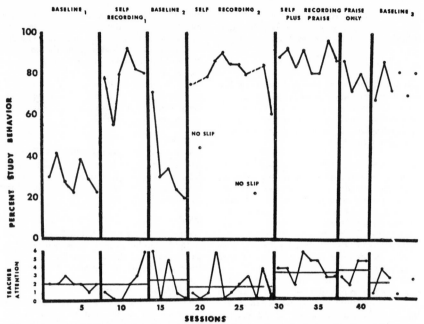

Fig. 2. A record of Liza's study behavior and/or teacher attention for study during: *Baseline₁*—before experimental procedures; *Self-Recording₁*—Liza recorded study or non-study on slips provided by counselor; *Baseline₂*—Self-recording slips withdrawn; *Self-Recording₂*—Self-recording slips reinstated; *Self-Recording Plus Praise*—Self-recording slips continued and teacher praise for study increased; *Praise Only*—Increased teacher praise maintained and self-recording withdrawn. *Baseline₃*—Teacher praise decreased to baseline levels.

a significant change in study behavior was noted. It increased to 78% and remained at that approximate level for the next six days. Teacher attention remained at a mean level of two times per session.

Baseline₂

On the fourteenth day of observation, Liza was told by the counselor that no more recording slips were available. The first day under these conditions the rate of study was 70%. It then dropped to an average of 27% for the next four days. Teacher attention averaged 2.5 times per session.

Self-Recording₂

When recording slips were again issued to Liza her study rate increased to an average of 80%. However, when on two days no slips were issued (Days 20 and 27) the rate declined to 30% and 22% respectively. During this phase, the teacher gave Liza attention approximately 1.7 times per class session.

Self-Recording Plus Praise

On Day 30, the teacher was again asked to praise Liza or give her increased attention when she studied. At this point the teacher agreed to do so because Liza was now engaging in a higher rate of study and he felt it would be easy and justifiable to do so. In this phase, teacher attention increased to 3.5 times per session. Liza continued to carry slips to class, sometimes filling them out and sometimes not. Under these conditions study increased to 88%.

Praise Only

On Day 38 the Praise Only phase was begun and slips discontinued. Teacher attention was observed to be at a mean rate of 3.7 times per session. Liza's study rate averaged 77%.

40

Table 1

Baseline₃

The teacher was then asked to decrease the amount of attention to Liza. During this Baseline₃ phase, no marked decrease in study rate was evident, though there was some decline. The first three joined points of the Baseline₃ phase represent consecutive days following the Praise Only phase. The three separated points represent post check days with approximately one-week intervals between observations, which further indicates increased study was being maintained.

Subject's Record Vs. Observer's Record

Table I presents the levels of study recorded by Liza and the observer during the Self-Recording phases. During the Self-Recording₁ phase, Liza recorded study or nonstudy on the average of 12 times per session. There was very little correlation between Liza's and the observer's estimates of the per cent of study on a day-to-day basis. Variations between records ranged up to 29%. However, the means of the overall subject-observer records were similar. For example, the mean of Liza's estimate of her study behavior during Baseline was 76%. The observer's record revealed that Liza actually studied an average of 78% of the time.

During the Self-Recording₂ phase, the number of times Liza recorded decreased to 11 marks per class. On four days she did not record at all. Liza's mean estimate of her study was 81%, the observer's was 80%. Again, there was little correlation between Liza's record and the observer's record on a day-to-day basis.

The number of times Liza recorded during the Self-Recording Plus Praise condition declined markedly to 2.3 times per session and Liza recorded on only three of the nine days during this experimental phase. Liza's mean estimate of study was 89%, that of the observer was 88%.

There was, of course, no self-recording during the other phases of the experiment.

EXPERIMENT II

Subject and Setting

The second subject, Stu, was an eighth-grade boy enrolled in a fifth-period math class at the same school. He was referred by his

Table 1

A record of per cent of study recorded by the observer and by Liza during self-recording phases of Exp. I.

EXPERIMENTAL PHASE	OBSERVER	LIZA
SELF-RECORDING₁	78 %	80%
	54 %	70%
	79 %	- -
	92 %	63%
	82 %	79%
	80 %	90%
MEAN	78 %	76 %
SELF-RECORDING₂	75 %	60%
PROBE "A"		
	78 %	100%
	87 %	80%
	90 %	FORGOT
	64 %	FORGOT
	84 %	FORGOT
	79 %	75%
PROBE "B"		
	83 %	90 %
	59 %	FORGOT
MEAN	80%	81%
SELF-RECORDING₃ PLUS PRAISE	89 %	FORGOT
	93 %	FORGOT
	83 %	FORGOT
	92 %	FORGOT
	81 %	66 %
	81 %	100 %
	96 %	FORGOT
	88 %	100 %
MEAN	88%	89%

teacher, a man, who expressed a desire to find some means to "shut Stu up". He reportedly talked out in class continually, disturbing both the teacher and his classmates. The class was composed of 28 "low" achieving students. It met for 25 min and then students went to lunch, returning afterward for another 20 min of class.

Observation

Observation records of Stu's behavior were made on sheets identical to those used in the previous experiment. The category of "talking out" was added, however, to the observation code. A talk out was defined as any verbalization that occurred during class which had not been recognized by the teacher and was recorded if it occurred at any time within each 10-sec interval. Since some of Stu's talk outs were not audible to the observer, both audible talk outs and instances when Stu's lips moved while facing another student and while another student was facing him were considered as talk outs. Study behavior and teacher attention to the subject were also recorded. Reliability of observation during each experimental phase was assessed in a manner similar to that used in the first study. Agreement of the records on the number of talk outs ranged from 84 to 100%.

METHOD

Baseline₁

For nine days before experimental procedures were initiated, data were recorded during the first half (Session A) of the period. On Days 1, 4, 5, 6, and 8 data were recorded during the second half of the period (Session B) as well.

Self-Recording, Session A

During the first experimental phase, the teacher handed a slip of paper to Stu at the beginning of class with the instructions to use it and that it would be collected during lunch. A facsimile of the slip is shown in Fig. 3. On it was printed a rectangular box about 2 by 5 in. (5 by 12.5 cm) and the statement "record a mark every time you talk out without permission". At the top of the slip was a place for the subject's name and the date. No further instructions were given.

Self-Recording, Session B

Slips were not issued during Session A but were given to Stu just before Session B. No contingencies were in effect during Session A.

Self-Recording (Sessions A and B)₁

Stu was given the slip at the beginning of class and told to record all period (both Session A and Session B). He was told the slip would be collected at the end of class.

Baseline₂

Self-recording slips were not issued for any part of the math period.

Self-Record (Sessions A and B)₂

Self-recording slips were issued and Stu was told to record talk outs for the entire period and that the slips would be collected at the end of class.

Fig. 3. Sample of self-recording sheet used by Stu.

RESULTS

Baseline₁

During the Baseline phase, Stu talked out on the average of 1.1 times per minute for the first half of the period and 1.6 times a minute during Session B. (See Fig. 4.)

Self-Recording, Session A

When the teacher began issuing slips to Stu for Session A, the frequency of his talk outs declined during Session A to 0.3 times a minute. The frequency of these talk outs during Session B, however, remained at 1.6 times a minute.

Self-Recording, Session B

After giving Stu the sheet seven days for Session A the teacher commented that "it is the second half of the period which has always been the problem", so contingencies were reversed. Slips were issued only during the second half of the period. The rate of verbalizing without permission during Session B declined to 0.5 times a minute. However, the rate of talking out during Session A, which was not under self-recording contingencies, increased to 1.2 times a minute.

Self-Recording (Sessions A and B)₁

When slips were issued for both A and B Sessions, the mean talk-out rate during A was 0.3 times per minute while that for B was 1.0 per minute, both well below baseline rates that were recorded.

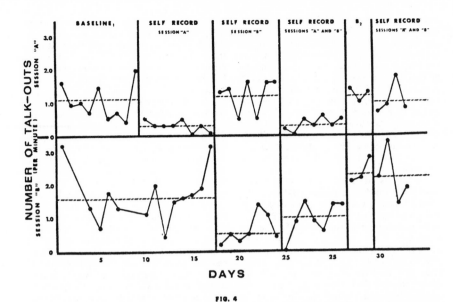

FIG. 4

Fig. 4. A record of Stu's talking-out behavior during Sessions A and B of fifth-period math class: *Baseline₁*—Before experimental procedures; *Self-Record, Session A*—Stu recorded his talk outs during Session A only; *Self-Record, Session B*—Stu recorded his talk outs during Session B only; *Self-Record, Sessions (A and B)₁*—Stu recorded his talk outs during both math class sessions; *Baseline₂*—Return to Baseline conditions, self-recording slips withdrawn; *Self-Record (A and B)₂*—Stu recorded his talk outs for both A and B Sessions.

Baseline₂

When slips were no longer furnished Stu during a second baseline phase, the rate of talk outs increased to a mean of 1.3 during Session A and 2.3 per minute during Session B.

Self-Recording (Sessions A and B)₂

When self-recording slips were again issued for the entire period, there was a slight but not significant decrease in the number of talk outs to a mean rate of 1.0 per minute in Session A and 2.2 per minute in Session B.

DISCUSSION

These studies indicated that it is possible to use self-recording procedures to modify behaviors of pupils in secondary-level public school classrooms. In Liza's case, self-recording was used to increase an appropriate behavior (study) while in Stu's case self-recording proved

effective in decreasing an inappropriate behavior (talking out).

In the experiment with Liza, someone outside the classroom, a counselor, was able to institute procedures that brought about an increase in study to a point that the teacher was able to maintain it with his attention and/or the other reinforcers already available in the classroom. Previous research had shown that systematic teacher attention can be used to increase study rates of elementary pupils (Hall, et al., 1968; Hall, et al., 1968). Broden and Hall (1968) demonstrated that teacher attention was also effective at the junior high school level. There were indications, however, that secondary level teachers were sometimes reluctant to carry out procedures that did not seem to fit their teaching style.

In Liza's case, initially the teacher did not feel that he could systematically increase his attention for study due to the lecture-discussion format he used. On the first day of Baseline₂, however, when the self-recording slips had been withdrawn, Liza's study behavior had remained at a high level. An analysis of the data showed that she had received an uncharacteristically high rate of attention from the teacher on that day (five times). This indicated that it might eventually be possible to withdraw the slips and maintain high study rates and that the teacher might willingly increase his attention to Liza for study if her study rate was already at a high level. The drop in study rate on the second day and subsequent days of Baseline$_2$ indicated that Liza was still very much under the control of self-recording.

The effects of issuing self-recording slips was further confirmed in the Self-Recording$_2$ phase. When probes were inserted and she was given no slips on Days 20 and 27 there were accompanying drops in study rates on those days. It is of interest to note that study dropped on Day 27 despite the fact that by this second probe, Liza had begun "forgetting" to record her study and non-study behavior on some days. This would indicate the possibility that the slip itself had become a cue or discriminative stimulus (S^D) for study whether or not it was used for self-recording. Liza's record of her study behavior did not correlate with the observer's record. However, it is important to note that correlation between Liza's estimate and her actual behavior was not necessary to achieve or maintain high study rates.

When the slips were withdrawn in the Praise Only phase, study was maintained at an acceptable level. Even when increased praise was withdrawn in the Baseline$_3$ phase, study remained at acceptable levels. Although it would have been interesting to have continued the Baseline$_3$ phase for a longer period the experiment was terminated due to the close of the school term. Even so, the data indicated that once higher study levels were achieved and maintained for a period of time, slips and high rates of teacher attention could be withdrawn without significant reductions in study. There was some subjective evidence that Liza's increased study may have resulted in increased academic performance because her report card grade in history increased from D— to C.

Although the experiment with Stu was in many ways a replication of the first study there were several important differences. Liza had expressed a desire, in fact had requested help, to improve her study behavior. Her counselor praised her when she reported high study rates on the self-recording slips. Later, her teacher began attending to her and praising her for study once higher rates were achieved.

Stu, on the other hand, had not expressed concern or asked for help in decreasing his talking-out behavior. The teacher rather than a counselor was the agent for dispensing the self-recording slips to Stu. Another difference was that no attempt was made to differentially reinforce Stu with praise or attention for the decreases in talking out that were observed. Previous research (Hall, Fox, Willard, Goldsmith, Emerson, Owen, Davis, and Porcia, 1970) indicates that doing so would have increased the effectiveness of the procedures used. In spite of these factors it seems that initially issuing slips and having Stu record on them did affect his talking-out behavior. As in Liza's case, this was true even though there was very little correlation between the number of talk outs recorded by Stu and the observer's record. This is illustrated by the fact that on Days 10, 11, and 12 the observer's record showed that Stu's talk outs were occurring at 0.4, 0.3, and 0.3 times per minute. On the same days however, Stu recorded 1.5, 0.5, and 0.8 talk outs per minute. That self-recording had little effect during the final phase of the experiment may have been due to the fact that no contingencies were ever applied to differential rates of talking out and the slips thus lost their effectiveness. Further research will be necessary to determine if this is the case. Furthermore, the records kept of his study behavior indicated that initially self-recording of talk outs may have affected his overall study rate. This effect was not conclusive or lasting, however. When self-recording was instituted for Session A, study increased from 30% to 55%. When self-recording was instituted for Session B, study increased from 24% to 42% while it decreased to 32% in Session A. When self-recording was instituted for the entire period, however, study decreased to 24%.

Perhaps the most promising feature of self-recording will be to use it as a procedure for initiating desirable levels of appropriate behavior to a point where the teacher can more easily reinforce the desired behavior with attention, praise, grades, or other reinforcers available in the classroom.

REFERENCES

Barrish, H., Saunders, M., and Wolf, M. M. Good behavior game: effects of individual contingencies for group consequences on disruptive behavior in a regular classroom. *Journal of Applied Behavior Analysis*, 1969, 2, 119-124.

Broden, M. and Hall, R. V. *Effects of teacher attention on the verbal behavior of two junior highschool pupils*. Paper presented at Council for Exceptional Children Convention, New York, 1968.

Broden, M., Hall, R. V., Dunlap, A., and Clark, R. Effects of teacher attention and a token reinforcement system in a junior highschool special education class. *Exceptional Children*, 1970, 36, 341-349.

Evans, G. and Oswalt, G. Acceleration of academic progress through the manipulation of peer influence. *Behaviour Research and Therapy*, 1967, 5, 1-7.

Hall, R. V. and Broden, M. Behavior changes in brain-injured children through social reinforcement. *Journal of Experimental Child Psychology*, 1967, 5, 463-479.

Hall, R. V., Fox, R., Willard, D., Goldsmith, L., Emerson, M., Owen, M., Davis, F., and Porcia, E. The teacher as observer and experimenter in the modification of disputing and talking out behaviors. *Journal of Applied Behavior Analysis*, 1971, 4, 141-149.

Hall, R. V., Lund, D., and Jackson, D. Effects of teacher attention on study behavior. *Journal of Applied Behavior Analysis*, 1968, 1, 1-12.

Hall, R. V., Panyan, M., Rabon, D., and Broden, M. Teacher applied contingencies and appropriate classroom behavior. *Journal of Applied Behavior Analysis*, 1968, 1, 315-322.

Madsen, C., Jr., Becker, W., and Thomas, D. Rules, praise, and ignoring: elements of elementary classroom control. *Journal of Applied Behavior Analysis*, 1968, 1, 139-150.

McKenzie, H., Clark, M., Wolf, M., Kothers, R., and Benson, C. Behavior modification of children with learning disabilities using grades as tokens and allowances as backup reinforcers. *Exceptional Children*, 1968, 34, 745-753.

Thomas, D., Becker, W., and Armstrong, M. Production and elimination of disruptive classroom behavior by systematically varying teacher's behavior. *Journal of Applied Behavior Analysis*, 1968, 1, 35-45.

Zimmerman, E. and Zimmerman, J. The alteration of behavior in a special classroom situation. *Journal of the Experimental Analysis of Behavior*, 1962, 5, 59-60.

CLASSROOM APPLICATIONS OF SELF-DETERMINED REINFORCEMENT

E. L. GLYNN

There is confusion in the thinking of educators on the use of extrinsic reinforcers in the control of children's classroom learning.

Clearly, educators do not object to extrinsic reinforcers *per se*, since grades, promotions, degrees, diplomas, and medals appear to enjoy the same widespread usage that Skinner noted in 1953. Moreover, it is difficult to imagine a classroom where teacher praise and reprimand are not used in an attempt to control children's behavior. Despite this widespread use of extrinsic reinforcement, there is objection to the employment of certain forms (such as candy and tokens) on the grounds that the student will become dependent on them and will be unable to perform without them. (Anderson, 1967.) Yet, surely, the same objection should hold against all forms of extrinsic reinforcement, including teacher praise and reprimand.

Perhaps an explanation for this confusion is that the operation of a token reinforcement system, more than the generally inconsistent operation of teacher praise and reprimand, emphasizes the extent to which children's behavior is under the control of an external agent. External control of behavior is distasteful to many educators who would agree with R. M. Gagné, that ". . . the student must be progressively weaned from dependence on the teacher or other agent external to himself." (Gagné 1965, p. 213.)

It is suggested that some of the confusion has resulted from equating extrinsic reinforcement with external control of behavior. The two terms are not interchangeable. Skinner (1953), in discussing self-control, suggests the individual may be capable of controlling his own behavior by means of dispensing his own reinforcement contingent upon making certain classes of responses. Various studies of self-reinforcement (Kanfer, Bradley, and Marston, 1962; Bandura and Kupers, 1964; and Bandura and Perloff, 1967), have permitted human subjects to take over the reinforcing function of the experimenter, by signalling correct responses, or rewarding themselves from a supply of tokens. Such self-administered reinforcing systems do seem to possess behavior maintenance capabilities, at least for simple responses—cranking a wheel (Bandura and Perloff, 1967), and visual discrimination (Kanfer and Duerfeldt, 1967).

The present study attempted to apply self-administered reinforcement procedures to classroom learning. If these procedures were to

Research reported in this paper was carried out in partial fulfillment of the Ph.D. degree at the Ontario Institute for Studies in Education (University of Toronto). The author is indebted to his chairman, Dr. S. B. K. Henderson for his valued support and encouragement.

JOURNAL OF APPLIED BEHAVIOR ANALYSIS, 1970, Vol. 3, pp. 123-132.

prove effective, they may be more acceptable to educators because they suggest a way to wean children from dependence on an external agent, and at the same time, would permit the use of effective extrinsic reinforcers.

Three major purposes of the study were: (1) to compare the effectiveness of self-determined and experimenter-determined token reinforcement treatments in the classroom setting; (2) to examine the effects of token withdrawal following these treatments; and (3) to examine the effect of differential token reinforcement experience on the amount of subsequent self-determined token reinforcement. A distinction is made here between *determination* and *administration* of reinforcement. All token reinforcement in this study was self-administered, but the amount of reinforcement was experimenter-determined, chance-determined, or self-determined (within the limits imposed by the experimental procedure).

METHOD

Experimental Situation

The study was planned to require a minimum of accommodation on the part of teacher and children, since it was intended to test the practicability of token reinforcement within the regular classroom program. The study did not require the teacher to alter subject content or teaching methods. Four intact class groups were used, which meant that no changes in timetable were requested, and children were never removed from their usual class setting. The subject matter, history and geography, was taught to all four classes, in the same topical order, by the one teacher. The token reinforcement treatments were administered by one experimenter in all four classes.

Subjects

One hundred and twenty-eight ninth-grade girls, in four classes in a Toronto Separate School, served as subjects. Class size ranged from 30 to 34. Girls had been assigned to classes from an alphabetic list, which was divided into four sections. While not truly random, this procedure at least precluded deliberate stratification of classes according to ability.

None of the children presented any problem to the teacher with regard to disruptive behavior. The teacher considered all children

"well-motivated" to learn, and interested in the subject matter. Having been present for a portion of the history and geography lessons of all four classes for the baseline period, the experimenter shared these opinions with the teacher.

Dependent Variables

1. Test performance. Working from a list of history and geography topics supplied by the teacher, the experimenter prepared 40 reading sheets, each of approximately 500 words. The class history and geography texts provided source material. Accompanying each reading sheet was a sheet of 20 five-option multiple-choice questions, based on the factual content of the reading sheets. Hence, the major dependent variable for each of the five phases of the study was the average number of test items correctly answered by each girl.

An attempt was made to match the readings and tests closely with the teacher's program. This was not always achieved because of the occasional need for the teacher to revise a topic before going on to the next, and because the experimenter was requested to produce several readings on New Zealand, at a time when the teacher had almost completed her coverage of the topic. The four classes received all readings and tests, in the same order, with each phase of the study containing approximately five history and five geography readings.

2. Performance-token ratios. The tokens were slips of paper, 2 by 1 in. (5 by 2.5 cm) bearing a star and the words "one credit". Tokens were exchanged for a variety of inexpensive prizes at the end of the first token phase, and at the end of the study. After each token reinforcement phase, a performance-token ratio was obtained for every girl. This ratio was formed by computing the total number of correct test items obtained in a particular phase, and dividing this number by the total number of tokens received in that phase.

Originally, it was planned to make the tokens exchangeable for the potentially reinforcing events available within the school program, and selected by children according to preference. Examples of such potentially reinforcing events are: time off a particular activity, library time, free time, homework exemptions, punishment exemptions, and the right to perform special duties. However, it was discovered that control of such events was out of the hands of the teacher concerned. Secondary school teachers do not have the same freedom in manipulating timetables and reinforcing events as do elementary school teachers, where one teacher handles one class for almost all the academic program.

In view of this difficulty, it was decided to provide a series of prizes, which could be obtained by turning in credits. An opportunity was taken to make the prizes relevant to some of the history and geography material, by using numerous inexpensive New Zealand souvenir items. When turning in their tokens, the girls were allowed to select a prize from the many items displayed, according to their rank order in number of tokens earned. There was a sufficient range of prizes for even the last-ranked child to have some choice.

3. Inter-class communication. An attempt was made to measure the extent of inter-class communication that occurred during the study, since it was realized that performance of one class could also be influenced by the knowledge that other classes were receiving different treatments. A set of three open-ended questions was administered to all children at the end of the study, asking them whether the treatment given their own class differed from that given the other classes, and if so, to state how.

Procedure

1. First baseline phase (Baseline I). This was a two-week period that served to establish basal measures of test performance in each of the four classes, and to accustom the children to the presence of the experimenter and the testing procedures. No tokens were issued.

Each day, the children were given a passage to read for 3 min, immediately after which the passage was collected, and a further 3 min were allowed for the multiple-choice test. (In considering these short time limits, it should be noted that the material encountered on the reading sheets would also have been covered by current teacher lessons). When the 3-min test session was over, immediate feedback of results was given, by means of the experimenter reading out the letter code for correct answers. The children then counted the number of test items correct, and entered this on a slip of paper in individual envelopes supplied for the purpose. Finally, test sheets and en-velopes were collected by the experimenter. Instructions stressed that information in the envelopes would not be made available to anyone other than the experimenter.

2. First token phase (Token I). This was the only period in which token reinforcement procedures differed across classes. The procedures employed were:

(a) Experimenter-determined token reinforcement. Under this treatment, children received tokens according to an explicit rate of one token per four correct answers. During the token reinforcement periods, five tokens were placed in each envelope each day. The children were instructed to calculate the number of tokens earned by dividing their test score by four. An arbitrary rule permitted the taking of an additional token for a fractional number. (Thus a child would take four tokens if the number earned were $3\frac{1}{4}$, $3\frac{1}{2}$, or $3\frac{3}{4}$.)

(b) Self-determined token reinforcement treatment. Under this treatment, children were invited to: "decide how many tokens you think you should award yourself. You can decide on any number from zero to five." No rules or suggestions were made concerning bases for decision making. The use of envelopes was intended to minimize the effect of social cues from peers, and of modeling peer standards, both of which are known to influence the rate of self-reinforcement (Marston, 1964; Bandura and Whalen, 1966; McMains and Liebert, 1968).

(c) Chance-determined token reinforcement. This was, in effect, an incentive-control treatment. Throughout the first token phase, the total number of tokens received by this class was kept identical with that of the self-reinforced class. Each day, chance-reinforced children were randomly assigned a "partner" from among the self-reinforced children. Regardless of performance of the chance-reinforced child, she found in her envelope the number of tokens that her self-reinforced "partner" for the day had taken. As well as providing an incentive control treatment, this procedure enabled the examination of the effect of such inconsistent experience of amount of reinforcement on extent of subsequent self-reinforcement.

(d) No-token reinforcement treatment. No token reinforcement was given under this treatment. The procedure was exactly the same as during Baseline I.

3. First token withdrawal phase (Withdrawal I). During this phase, token reinforcement was withdrawn from experimenter-reinforced, self-reinforced, and chance-reinforced classes.

4. Second token phase (Token II). Tokens were reintroduced for the experimenter-reinforced, self-reinforced, and chance-reinforced classes, but all three classes were now permitted to operate the self-reinforced procedure. The major question asked was whether the children previously reinforced according to an externally imposed standard (experimenter-reinforced) would subsequently display a rate of self-reinforcement close to this standard.

5. Second baseline phase (Baseline II). During this phase, the baseline readings and tests were readministered, in order to compare increase in performance on re-learning among the four classes. Tokens were withdrawn for the first half (Withdrawal II), but included for the second half (Token III).

6. Review test. A review test was constructed of items from each of the tests administered during the first token phase, the token withdrawal, and the second token phase, in order to determine whether treatment effects were of a long-term nature. Since the test was administered after the repeat of baseline, the test-retest interval was 2 to 4 weeks for items from the second token phase (Sections C), 4 to 6 weeks for items from the token withdrawal phase (Section B), and 6 to 8 weeks for items from the first token phase (Section A). For the review test, seven tokens were provided in the envelopes of the experimenter-reinforced, self-reinforced, and chance-reinforced classes, and the self-reinforced procedure was applied in all three classes.

RESULTS

Daily test performance scores of all classes throughout the study are listed in Table 1. Also shown are the mean test performance scores for each phase of the study.

It was considered that the performance of the non-reinforced class provided the best available estimate of variations due to fluctuations in test difficulty. Accordingly, Fig. 1 was produced by depicting the daily performance of the three treatment classes, in terms of difference from the non-reinforced class, so that variation due to fluctuating test difficulty might be removed.

Baseline I

An analysis of variance performed on mean scores for Baseline I yielded a non-significant between-classes effect (F 3, 116 = 1.65, p > 0.05), and Hartley's test for homogeneity of variance yielded an F max. of 1.40 which is not significant. The four classes were thus regarded as being similar in performance during Baseline I.

Token I

An analysis of covariance was performed on Token I mean scores, using Baseline I mean scores as covariate. The between-classes effect was significant. (F 3, 115 = 16.69, p < 0.001). An analysis of variance for repeated-measures on test scores in every alternate session of the Token I phase yielded an insignificant classes-by-sessions interaction. (F 12, 464 = 1.61, p > 0.05). Hence, analyses of mean Token I scores do not conceal any useful information about differential performance of classes across sessions.

The significant between-classes effect noted above is evident in Fig. 1. Token I mean scores were adjusted for the effect of the covariate (Baseline I performance), by the method suggested by Winer (1962, p. 592). Comparisons were made among the adjusted means by the Newman-Keuls procedure. The experimenter-reinforced and self-reinforced classes did not differ from one another, nor did the non-reinforced and chance-reinforced classes differ from one another. However, both the experimenter-reinforced and the self-reinforced classes differed significantly from the non-reinforced and chance-reinforced classes. The self-determined reinforcement procedure was equally as effective as the externally determined one, in producing an increase in performance.

Withdrawal I

The analysis of covariance performed on Withdrawal I mean scores (using Baseline I mean scores as covariate), yielded a significant between-classes effect (F 3, 115 = 3.24, p < 0.05), though the effect was weaker than that of Token I. This was expected, since in Token I, performance was directly influenced by differences in treatment procedures. Again, a repeated-measures analysis of variance yielded a non-significant classes-by-sessions interaction

49

Table 1
Mean Performance Scores for all Sessions and Phases

Session		Non-Reinforced	Chance-Reinforced	Experimenter-Reinforced	Self-Reinforced
				Class	
Baseline I:	1	10.60*	9.57	9.88	9.66
	2	11.60*	10.54	11.13	11.47
	3	9.69*	8.80	8.70	8.35
	4	9.82	8.63	8.91	9.91*
	5	10.71*	10.19	9.47	8.70
	6	12.21*	10.87	9.81	10.69
	7	9.72*	6.97	8.39	9.25
	8	10.55*	9.32	9.81	9.70
	9	9.46*	6.55	7.44	7.25
	10	9.63	9.42	8.78	9.97*
	Mean:	10.38*	9.02	9.13	9.47
Token I:	11	7.44	7.14	8.33*	8.33*
	12	10.08	9.37	11.29*	10.15
	13	9.38	9.53	11.08	12.66*
	14	10.30	9.37	11.32	11.45*
	15	8.07	6.28	9.14	10.14*
	16	10.53	10.41	11.62	12.54*
	17	9.57	8.07	10.32*	10.07
	18	11.50	11.33	13.97*	13.27
	19	11.17	11.13	12.41	12.56*
	20	10.07	10.09	12.06*	11.61
	Mean:	9.71	9.13	11.12*	11.09
Withdrawal I:	21	11.25	9.20	11.61*	10.67
	22	10.53	8.75	10.52	11.10*
	23	12.83*	12.52	12.75	12.39
	24	13.31	13.79	13.63	14.48*
	25	11.29	10.86	10.94	12.73*
	26	8.44*	7.39	8.44*	7.40
	27	10.62*	9.46	9.74	10.23
	28	10.31*	8.87	10.13	8.80
	29	10.69	10.03	9.70	11.23*
	30	8.59*	6.83	8.55	8.32
	Mean:	10.44	9.72	10.53	10.87*
Token II:	31	11.12*	9.42	9.48	10.16
	32	11.97	10.55	11.84	12.28*
	33	9.89*	8.58	9.48	9.33
	34	11.47	10.42	11.63*	11.10
	35	9.17	8.10	9.52	9.87*
	36	11.50	9.46	11.28	13.22*
	37	8.36	7.52	8.76	9.13*
	38	9.63	8.83	11.03*	9.38
	39	9.83	10.34	11.10	12.16*
	40	12.30	11.45	12.65*	11.80
	Mean:	10.47	9.33	10.64*	10.59
Baseline II:					
(a) Withdrawal II:	41	10.90	11.42	12.42	12.70*
	42	13.64	12.55	13.84	14.09*
	43	10.36*	8.13	10.06	10.00
	44	8.36	9.97	10.91*	10.90
	45	11.57	10.40	11.25	11.07
	Mean:	10.74	10.49	11.79	11.87*
(b) Token III:	46	11.38	11.04	12.78	13.19*
	47	10.29	9.50	10.42*	10.10
	48	10.72	10.72	10.83	11.57*
	49	10.59*	8.93	9.37	9.83
	50	11.14	10.41	11.23	12.35*
	Mean:	10.48	9.78	10.89	10.96*

*Indicates highest scoring class.

(F 12, 464 = 1.17, p > 0.05) so that analyses of mean scores for Withdrawal I did not conceal information about differential performance of classes across sessions. The significant effect reported above suggests that there remained some effects of Token I treatments during

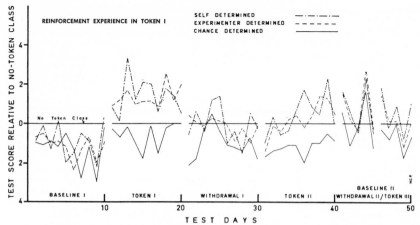

Fig. 1. Daily test performance of the three token classes relative to the no-token class.

Withdrawal I. This can be seen in Fig. 1. After the mean scores from Withdrawal I had been adjusted for the effect of the covariate, Newman-Keuls comparisons were made among them. It was found that the experimenter-reinforced and self-reinforced classes performed better than the non-reinforced class, but not better than the chance-reinforced class.

Token II

The analysis of covariance performed on Token II mean scores (using Baseline I mean scores as covariate) yielded a significant, though weak, between-classes effect (F 3, 115 = 2.85, $p < 0.05$), but none of the possible comparisons among adjusted means yielded significant differences at the 0.05 level by Newman-Keuls tests. However, it can be seen from Fig. 1 that the experimenter-reinforced and self-reinforced classes were superior to the non-reinforced class for the greater part of Token II, while the chance-reinforced class always remained inferior to the non-reinforced class, suggesting some differences in performance between classes.

A repeated-measure analysis of variance of Token II data yielded a significant classes-by-sessions interaction (F 12, 464 = 2.47, $p < 0.01$). Hence, Token II mean scores obscure differential performance of classes across sessions. Figure 1 shows that the experimenter-reinforced and self-reinforced classes displayed a more obvious improvement in performance

relative to the non-reinforced class than did the chance-reinforced class.

Baseline II

As the readings and tests administered during Baseline II were the same as those for Baseline I, comparisons of performance gains over the two administrations were made across classes.

Highly significant phase effects were found, for both the Withdrawal II and Token III halves of the repeated-baseline tests, but these may be readily attributed to general practice effects. However, significant classes-by-phases interactions were also found: F 3, 116 = 4.23, $p < 0.01$ (for Withdrawal II), and F 3, 116 = 2.80, $p < 0.05$ (for Token III). Newman-Keuls comparison were carried out to examine these effects further. Table 2 shows that the inter-

Table 2
Newman-Keuls qr Values for Differences between Baseline I and Baseline II Mean Test Performance Scores.

Test Days	Class	Baseline I	Baseline II	qr
1-5	NR	10.49	10.74	0.84
and	YR	9.43	10.49	3.53
41-45	ER	9.55	11.79	7.42**
	SR	9.49	11.87	7.86**
6-10	NR	9.84	10.48	1.77
and	YR	8.58	9.78	3.32
46-50	ER	8.66	10.89	6.18**
	SR	8.81	10.96	5.96**

**$p < 0.01$

51

action effect is attributable to significant increases on Baseline II administration for the experimenter-reinforced and self-reinforced classes. This increase is not significant in the case of the non-reinforced and chance-reinforced classes.

Review Test

Analysis of variance performed on scores from each section of the Review Test yielded a significant between-classes effect (F 3, 108 = 4.47, p < 0.01) for Token I items (Section A). Newman-Keuls comparisons of class means revealed a pattern of significant results parallel to that of Token I performance. On Section A items, both the experimenter-reinforced and self-reinforced classes (x = 9.89 and 9.71) were slightly better than the non-reinforced and chance-reinforced classes (x = 8.21 and 8.00). There was no significant difference between the self-reinforced and experimenter-reinforced classes, nor between the non-reinforced and chance-reinforced classes. The performance increments resulting from differential reinforcement schedules evidently have some permanence. Sections B and C of the Review Test (Withdrawal I and Token II items) yielded no between-classes effects that reflected earlier treatments.

Performance-Token Ratios

Table 3 presents data concerning number of tokens taken, and performance-token ratios of the three token classes throughout the study.

Analysis of variance indicated no significant differences in number of tokens taken by the three classes during Token I (F 2, 90 = 0.453, p > 0.25). Hence, amount of token reinforcement can be regarded as similar across classes. Token I performance-token ratios were subjected to analysis by a median test for independent groups (Hays, 1962), since variances

for the three groups departed widely from homogeniety (F max. 3, 30 = 9.05, p < 0.01). The observed Chi-squared value for the median test was 35.1 (p < 0.001). Hence, despite similarity of amount of token reinforcement during the Token I phase, the performance-token ratio for the self-reinforced class was higher than those of the experimenter-reinforced and chance-reinforced classes, indicating that the self-reinforced class had "worked hardest" per token.

Similar results emerged in Token II. Again, no significant difference in amount of token reinforcement was found (F 2, 90 = 2.37, p > 0.05), but significant differences were found in performance-token ratios, (F 2, 90 = 3.18, p < 0.05), with that of the self-reinforced class being higher than those of the experimenter-reinforced or chance-reinforced classes.

In Token III, analysis of variance revealed that classes did differ in terms of amount of token reinforcement taken (F 2, 90 = 4.19, p < 0.05) with the self-reinforced class taking fewer tokens than the experimenter-reinforced class, though more than the chance-reinforced class. Yet, as Table 3 shows, the self-reinforced class again displayed the highest performance-token ratio.

The above pattern of results was also found in the data from the Review Test. There were significant differences both in amount of token reinforcement taken by the three classes (F 2, 81 = 62.59, p < 0.001), and in the performance-token ratios (F 2, 81 = 9.20, p < 0.001). It can be seen from Table 3 that the self-reinforced class again took fewer tokens than the experimenter-reinforced and chance-reinforced classes, and displayed the highest performance-token ratio on the Review Test.

Table 4 supplies information on the variability in performance-token ratios for all token reinforcement phases. Clearly, the ex-

Table 3

Number of Tokens Taken and Performance-Token Ratios in all Token Phases

Phase	Chance-Reinforced Class		Experimenter-Reinforced Class		Self-Reinforced Class	
	Number	Ratio	Number	Ratio	Number	Ratio
Token I	2.87	3.26	3.10	3.60	2.90	3.99
Token II	2.63	3.54	3.13	3.43	2.76	3.92
Token III	2.83	3.71	3.29	3.33	2.95	3.89
Review Test	3.82	7.77	5.82	5.77	3.57	9.50

Table 4
Standard Deviations of Performance-Token Ratios

Phase	Chance Reinforced Class	Experimenter- Reinforced Class	Self- Reinforced Class
Token I	0.98	0.43	1.31
Token II	1.01	0.59	0.63
Token III	1.12	0.62	0.76
Review Test	3.86	1.86	3.69

perimenter-reinforced class displayed the least variability throughout.

Communication Between Classes

On the open-ended questions concerning knowledge of the treatment of other classes, the maximum "information score" was 3.0. Mean scores for the four classes were: non-reinforced, 0.74; chance-reinforced, 0.73; experimenter-reinforced, 0.44; and self-reinforced, 0.27. Newman-Keuls comparisons showed the self-reinforced class mean to be significantly lower than those of the chance-reinforced and non-reinforced classes. This could indicate that reported performance differences might be confounded by other factors arising from amount of information about other classes. However, a detailed examination of responses to the open-ended questions suggested that the extent of any such confounding was not great. Children made surprisingly few statements about how procedures in any of the classes had differed from their own.

DISCUSSION

1. Effectiveness of Self-Determined Reinforcement

Restrictions must be placed on generalizing from the findings of this study, both in terms of the particular children involved, and in terms of the narrow range for self-determined reinforcement permitted by the procedure. It is an open question as to whether these results would be replicated with younger or underpriviledged children, without some modification of procedure—for example, providing a wider variety of more meaningful prizes. It is also an open question as to whether similar results would have been obtained with these children, had there been wider limits allowed on amount of reinforcement, and had there been no check by the experimenter on the amount of reinforcement taken. Furthermore,

these results would appear more convincing, had there been a further non-reinforced control class at another school. This would have yielded direct information about the effect on the non-reinforced class, of knowledge of reinforcement contingencies in the other classes. More accurately than the self-report measures used in this study, it would determine whether the performance of the non-reinforced class during token phases, was, in fact, only a reflection of test difficulty, or whether it was confounded with adverse motivational effects arising from knowledge of other treatments.

Nevertheless, the study does suggest that the concept of self-determined reinforcement is both applicable and appropriate for studies of academic performance in the classroom. Self-determined reinforcement, within the above-mentioned limits, proved to be at least as equally effective as experimenter-determined reinforcement, in terms of improving academic performance. Children were able to control successfully the token reinforcement for their classroom learning, when both social cues and specific instructions about extent of reinforcement were minimized. It would seem that the notion of systematic social reinforcement as a "critical component" of an effective token system (Kuypers, Becker, and O'Leary, 1968) may need to be qualified.

It is clear that token reinforcement procedures were less effective in Token II and Token III than in Token I. Since tokens were exchanged for prizes for the first time at the end of Token I, and since identical sets of prizes were available at the end of Token III, it is thought that the tokens dropped much of their value as reinforcers. There is a need for future studies to ensure a sufficiently varied set of reinforcing events to back up the tokens. The particular prizes used in this study were nevertheless effective during Token I, possibly because of their novelty.

2. Performance of the Chance-Reinforced Treatment Class

This class performed at a level generally below that of the non-reinforced class throughout the study. The inconsistent experience of this class in terms of amount of reinforcement during the Token I phase, seems to have not only precluded performance increments during this phase, but also to have prevented subsequent self-determined reinforcement proce-

53

dures from having any incremental effect. This is certainly an indication that the ability to apply self-determined reinforcement is strongly influenced by the standards of externally determined reinforcement previously experienced. Hence, inconsistency of reinforcement can occur not only in terms of interpersing reinforcement with non-reinforcement as consequences of a given behavior, but also in terms of unpredictable amounts of reinforcement for a given behavior. These results suggest that parents and teachers, who function as major external reinforcing agents for children's behavior, should be aware that one consequence of maintaining such inconsistent standards of reinforcement may be impairment of the child's ability to apply self-determined reinforcement procedures effectively. If such an ability is considered as one component of self-control, as Marston and Kanfer (1963) suggest, then inconsistent experiences of amount of reinforcement would have a debilitating effect on the development of an individual's ability to control his own behavior.

3. Withdrawal of Tokens

Findings suggest that after token withdrawal, the four classes did not revert to the similarity of performance displayed during the baseline. Token reinforcement classes experimenter-reinforced and self-reinforced remained slightly superior to the non-reinforced class. There seems little evidence to justify the fear that children would become dependent upon token reinforcement so as to be unable to perform without it.

4. Performance-Token Ratios

Data on performance-token ratios provide further support that the operation of self-determined reinforcement is influenced by standards of externally determined reinforcement previously experienced. Table 3 shows that the experimenter-reinforced class adhered more closely to the performance-token ratio experienced during the Token I phase than did either the self-reinforced or chance-reinforced class. The experimenter-reinforced class had been supplied with an explicit ratio, whereas the self-reinforced and chance-reinforced classes had not. Yet, the self-reinforced and chance-reinforced classes moved towards a much higher performance-token ratio, especially on the Review Test. Table 4 indicates

that the experimenter-reinforced class displayed the least variability in ratios throughout the study. This would be expected if members of this class were adhering to a common standard. The striking finding is that the children who had the greatest opportunity for leniency in taking tokens (self-reinforced class), actually imposed the strictest ratio on themselves.

The performance-token ratios observed in this study imply that an alternative to a teacher laying down explicit acceptable standards of performance for classroom learning, might be the provision of access to reinforcement on the basis of standards determined by individual children.

5. Applicability of Procedures

The token-reinforcement procedures employed proved to be well suited to classroom use. Tokens did not have to be paid out individually to each child (a saving of time and energy for the teacher). Handing out the envelopes took about 1 min each day, and children took about the same time to take their tokens and return the envelopes. Since envelopes contained a slip bearing daily performance scores, a continuous record was available showing performance and number of tokens taken. For experimental purposes, it can be noted that by including differential instructions in envelopes, several reinforcement procedures might be operated simultaneously.

REFERENCES

Anderson, R. C. Educational Psychology. *Annual Review of Psychology*, 1967, **18**, 129-164.
Bandura, A. and Kupers, C. J. Transmission of self-reinforcement through modeling. *Journal of Abnormal and Social Psychology*, 1964, **69**, 1-9.
Bandura, A. and Whalen, C. K. The influence of antecedent reinforcement and divergent modeling cues on patterns of self reward. *Journal of Personality and Social Psychology*, 1966, **3**, 373-382.
Bandura, A. and Perloff, B. Relative efficiency of self-monitored and externally imposed reinforcement systems. *Journal of Personality and Social Psychology*, 1967, **7**, 111-116.
Gagné, R. M. *The conditions of learning.* New York: Holt, Rinehart & Winston, 1965.
Kanfer, F. H., Bradley, M. M., and Marston, A. R. Self-reinforcement as a function of degree of learning. *Psychological Reports*, 1962, **10**, 885-886.
Kanfer, F. H. and Duerfeldt, P. H. Motivational properties of self-reinforcement. *Perceptual and Motor Skills*, 1967, **25**, 237-246.

Kuypers, D. S., Becker, W. C., and O'Leary, K. D.   How to make a token system fail. *Exceptional Children,* October 1968, 101-117.

Marston, A. R.   Variables affecting incidence of self-reinforcement. *Psychological Reports,* 1964, **14,** 879-884.

Marston, A. R. and Kanfer, F. H.   Human reinforcement: experimenter and subject controlled. *Journal of Experimental Psychology,* 1963, **66,** 91-94.

McMains, M. J. and Liebert, R. M.   Influence of discrepancies between successively modeled self-reward criteria on the adoption of a self-imposed standard. *Journal of Personality and Social Psychology,* 1968, **8,** 166-171.

Skinner, B. F.   *Science and human behavior.* New York: Macmillan, 1953.

Winer, B. J.   *Statistical principles in experimental design.* New York: McGraw-Hill, 1962.

SECTION TWO

CONTINGENCY CONTRACTING

A contract is an agreement between parties to do or not to do certain things. While contracting is not new in the business world, it is a relatively recent approach for managing adolescent behaviors. Nevertheless, the purpose of contracting, regardless of setting, is to assure the parties that their expectations will be met if their obligations are, in turn, fulfilled. Quid pro quo (from the Latin), meaning something for something, is the usual way of referring to these expectations and obligations.

Although some adults may not have been aware of it, or may yet deny it, they have never really expected something for nothing from children. Many parents, for example, have offered praise, encouragement, trips, and other goodies in order to receive desired behavior from their children. In return, the children may have spent long hours learning a difficult task. By the time these children have reached adolescence, they may have come to enjoy learning for learning's sake and, thus, might appear to be doing something for nothing. Not all adolescents have had the benefits of this early training, however. For these "deprived" adolescents, contracting is explicit assurance that they will receive something of value (e.g., free time) if they will perform a task (e.g., complete an English assignment) or give up some behavior (e.g., disruptive classroom behavior). For the adults involved, contracting is a clarification of their responsibilities to provide rewards in return for improved adolescent behaviors.

Contracting, of course, is more than an incentive system for deprived adolescents. Contracting provides practical experience for entering the world outside the home and school where contracts are an everyday occurrence. Greater understanding and respect for others may result from the mutual planning that goes into developing a contract. Perhaps the greatest value of all is that in contracting adults and adolescents are working cooperatively with each other in the management of behaviors. It appears that contracting has wide utility with students of vastly different characteristics. The Anandam and Williams study demonstrates that behavioral contracts are particularly effective in improving the academic and social skills of highly disruptive students. The study by Williams, Long, and Yoakley points out how contracting has application even for advantaged, well behaved students. The final article (MacDonald, Gallimore, and MacDonald) indicates that contracts can be used effectively outside the classroom setting to facilitate productive academic behaviors.

KAMALA ANANDAM

ROBERT L. WILLIAMS

A Model for Consultation with Classroom Teachers on Behavior Management

INCREASED attention is being given to the counselor's role as a consultant, in the controversy concerning the duties of a counselor (Dinkmeyer, 1968; Faust, 1968; Warters, 1964; Wrenn, 1962). The counselor's exclusive commitment to the counseling of pupils is being questioned by those with a sociological point of view. These individuals contend that if the counselor would work with the school's teaching and administrative staff to change sociological conditions within the school, many pupil problems now demanding counseling would not arise in the first place (Boy & Pine, 1969).

It is unfortunate that counseling and consulting are often considered incompatible (McGehearty, 1968). Weinberg (1968) affirms that counseling and consulting are both legitimate ways to help students who have prob-lems. The former is a psychological approach involving direct contact with the child and the latter is a sociological approach in which the resolution of students' problems entails restructuring of social variables in the classroom. The counselor would affect far more students by serving as a consultant to classroom teachers regarding appropriate modification of classroom conditions than he could possibly reach through individual counseling, thus maximizing his impact in the school. Consulting would also enable the counselor to modify variables in the classroom which otherwise would necessitate extensive therapeutic remediation in counseling.

Pupils who behave in aggressive, disruptive and/or other socially undesirable ways in school pose serious problems for their teachers. Disruptive classroom behavior is frequently

THE SCHOOL COUNSELOR, 1971, Vol. 18, pp. 253-259.

an outgrowth of frustrations a student experiences in the classroom milieu (Feldhusen, Thurston, & Benning, 1967). A student's disruptive behavior not only decreases his opportunity to learn, but also restricts the learning opportunities of other students. Furthermore, a disruptive student generally elicits much negative behavior from the teacher, which in turn increases the student's disruptive behavior. The student and the teacher are thus the victims of a vicious cycle.

This paper describes the consultative procedures used to alter teacher and student behaviors in a classroom initially characterized by a high degree of disruptive behavior. Since counseling with individual students is not always economically feasible, the experimenters used an approach that permitted the problems to be attacked on a group basis in the regular classroom (Quay, Werry, McQueen, & Sprague, 1966). The sample used was an eighth grade English class (N=30) in a racially mixed city high school located in an economically impoverished area of eastern Tennessee. The behavioral management technique incorporated in this consultative model is what the experimenters call "behavior contracting" to distinguish it from Homme's (1969) "contingency contracting" and Poppen and Thompson's (1970) "grade contracting." The success of similar behavior contracting with individual children has been demonstrated in the investigations of Cantrell, Cantrell, Huddleston, and Wooldridge (1969), Toews (1969), and Thompson (1970).

Method

The experimenters learned from the school counselor that one of the teachers had requested help in managing her class, which had become so unruly that she could not continue teaching. The consultation rendered to this counselor consisted of:

1. Meeting with the teacher to find out what behavior she considered inappropriate in the classroom and what behavior she would like to see her pupils exhibit.

2. Observing teacher and student behavior in the classroom in order to identify the contingencies leading to inappropriate behavior.

3. Conferring with the teacher to discuss possible ways to reduce inappropriate behavior.

4. Obtaining suggestions from students for eliminating inappropriate behavior.

5. Executing a plan of action derived from items 1 through 4.

6. Evaluating the effectiveness of the plan of action and making further recommendations.

Meeting with the Teacher

The first meeting with the teacher revealed that the students in this particular class were performing at different academic levels; that she was giving little individual assistance to students; that her attempts to explain subject matter to the class were regularly interrupted by students moving from their seats and talking to each other. She made reference to a girl (target subject) who talked incessantly during class. The teacher claimed she had tried all possible means to stop the girl's talking: changing her seat, making her stay after school, admonishing her in class, and giving her a writing assignment. None of these means was effective. The teacher asked the consultant to suggest ways to get the pupils to be quiet, stay in their seats, listen to her explanations, and do the assigned work in class. After the teacher requested help, the consultant asked for permission to enter the classroom to make some observations.

Observation in Class

The consultant observed the class for two days, using 10-second time intervals for recording behavior. In each time interval, the student was observed for five seconds and the teacher for five seconds. The behavior codes used for the observation are presented in Table 1. Observational data collected for the two class periods revealed that the target student was engaged in inappropriate behavior for 44 out of 59 time sample units on the first day and for 77 out of 83 units on the second day. However, several other students also exhibited disrup-

tive behavior during these two days. Observation of a randomly picked student on the first day showed that out of 60 time units he was engaged in inappropriate behavior for 43 units. On both days, the largest number of units of teacher behavior was observed in the "attention to kids" category (74 units). This behavior generally consisted of the teacher answering a student's question individually without involving other students or assigning them some work. Inattention to the other students seemed to elicit inappropriate behaviors. The next largest category of teacher behavior was "admonishing" the group (20 units). The most frequent admonitions were "Get busy," "Turn around and be quiet," "If you have nothing to do, be quiet," and "Come back to your seat." Admonitions were usually followed by inappropriate student behavior; in other words, the admonitions were obtaining the results opposite of what she desired.

Table 1

Codes and Categories of Behavior Used for Observation

Student behavior		Teacher behavior	
M	Moving out of seat without permission	Te	Teaching, looking at students
NO	Noise with objects	D	Desk work
OR	Orientation response	B	Board work
T	Talking	AD	Attending to individual students
BI	Behavior inappropriate, i.e., not doing what the teacher wants the class to do	A	Attending to student being observed
W	Writing	S	Looking at students in order to make them behave
R	Reading		
H	Hand raised	AG	Admonishing the group
L	Listening—neutral response	R	Positively reinforcing appropriate behavior
VR	Verbal response to teacher		
BA	Behavior appropriate, i.e., doing what the teacher wants the class to do		

60

Conferring with the Teacher

The consultant conferred with the teacher at the end of the two days. The observational data and other observational notes were explained to her. It became obvious to both the consultant and the teacher that the entire class needed help and not just the target student. The consultant suggested that a behavior contract or intra-group competition could be used to modify inappropriate behavior. The teacher felt that both methods would be appropriate for her class, since, in her opinion, some students did not care how they rated with the teacher.

Obtaining Students' Suggestions

In order to involve the students in formulating the contract, they were asked the following questions:

1. If you were a teacher, what rules would you make for your class?

2. What would you do if someone broke the rule?

3. If you were given free time in class, what would you like to do?

4. Whom would you like to have sit next to you in class? Give three choices.

In most instances, student responses to these questions corresponded to answers frequently given by teachers. For example, the two most frequently suggested rules were "Don't talk," and "Don't get up from seat." Most students indicated that if someone broke a rule he should stay after school, be sent to the principal, or be given a writing assignment. The three most popular free-time choices were reading (books and comics), talking, and drawing on the blackboard.

Plan of Action

A behavior contract was developed which incorporated the ideas of the students, teacher, and consultant. Teacher expectations for appropriate student behaviors such as (a) bringing paper, pencil, and required books; (b) taking a 5-point daily quiz; (c) completing the learning task assigned each day; and (d) taking a 30-point weekly test on Fridays were made explicit in the contract. A student earned points for emitting the appropriate behaviors and lost points for behavior such as disruptive talking. Grades were made contingent on the number of points accumulated by students and free time on the completion of the daily task. During free time, the students engaged in activities such as drawing, coloring, working puzzles, writing on the board, and reading comics. The teacher's gradebook was available for student examination any time during the class period.

Sociometric choices given by the students were used in modifying seating patterns, i.e., those who liked each other were seated in one row, with each row constituting a group. There was a total of five groups, with unequal numbers in each. The services of a senior student were made available to assist the teacher in correcting the daily test and in taking care of the reinforcement activities. Each row had a group leader who maintained the record of points earned and lost.

Results and Evaluation

Evaluation of the effectiveness of behavior contracting was based on four observations over the six weeks period (see Table 2). Appropriate student behavior greatly increased after introduction of the behavior contract.

The major changes observed in the teacher's behavior were that she stopped admonishing the group and began to positively reinforce students for their accomplishments (see Table 3). Instead of attempting to catch students misbehaving, she looked for hands raised soliciting help.

Records maintained by the student aide for 19 days indicated that an average of 15 students finished their assigned task every day and engaged in approximately 10 minutes of free time activity. It may be seen from the distribution of grades for the contracting period (third six weeks) as compared to that in the preceeding six weeks (see Table 4) that the classroom atmosphere improved through behavior contracting, which facilitates achievement or at least the teacher's evaluation of achievement.

Conclusions

The experimenters contend that one reason the teacher became more reinforcing after effecting the contract was because the contract markedly increased the number of behaviors that she could legitimately reinforce. The

Table 2

Summary of Student Behavior Before and During Contract Period

Observation	Student behavior units	
	Appropriate	Inappropriate
Before contract		
I (target)	15	44
II (target)	6	77
During contract		
III	116	50
IV	127	5
V	152	27
VI	142	29

Note: Behavior frequencies during the contract period are based on observation of the target and one randomly selected subject.

Table 3

Summary of Teacher Behavior for the Four Observations During Contract Period

Behavior category	Frequency of teacher behaviors preceding	
	Appropriate student behavior	Inappropriate student behavior
Teaching, looking at pupils	110	35
Desk work	35	12
Board work	27	3
Attending to individual students	305	48
Attending to student being observed	9	3
Looking for students with hands raised	17	7
Admonishing the students	0	0
Positively reinforcing for appropriate behavior	14	2

Table 4

Grade Distribution Before and
During Contract Period

Letter grade	2nd six weeks (before)	3rd six weeks (during)
A	0	1
B	3	8
C	6	8
D	10	10
F	11	3

students had participated in the formulation of the contract and knew exactly what behaviors were considered appropriate and inappropriate under the terms of the contract. The contract had given the teacher an efficient procedure (deducting points) of dealing with inappropriate behaviors, without having to admonish students. After introduction of the contract, inappropriate behaviors (e.g., failure to bring paper, pencils, and books and disruptive talking) were appreciably reduced. Such a dramatic change in student behaviors undoubtedly enables a teacher to have more positive feelings toward students and emit much more reinforcing behavior.

The philosophy underlying the contract system is that mutual respect between teacher and students assigns responsibility to each and demands certain commitment from each. Failure to meet the commitment entails the consequences listed in the contract. The arrangement permits the student to learn or not to learn without having to cope with the teacher's admonitions and nagging. This philosophy is by no means new to the galaxy of writings in the area of counseling (Glasser, 1969; Missildine,

1963; Rogers, 1969). What is new and unique is the technique of contracting which elicits behavior in tune with the basic philosophy.

The efforts toward better classroom atmosphere and better teaching situations do not stop with initially formulating the contract. Constant evaluations would indicate where revisions are required to increase the reinforcement value of the system to both teacher and students. For instance, the contract presented in this article was subsequently modified so that: (a) students could obtain points for completing the daily task, (b) recognition could be given in class for the best performing group every week, and (c) points earned by each student were posted each day on a wall chart for all members of the class to see. At the time this paper was prepared, it was too early to determine the long-range impact of the latter modifications, but the initial impact was almost to eliminate inappropriate behaviors and substantially increase appropriate behaviors.

References

Boy, A. V., & Pine, G. J. A sociological view of the counselor's role: A dilemma and a solution. *Personnel and Guidance Journal*, 1969, *47*, 736–740.

Cantrell, R. P., Cantrell, M. L., Huddleston, C. M., & Wooldridge, R. L. Contingency contracting with school problems, *Journal of Applied Behavior Analysis*, 1962, *2*, 215–220.

Dinkmeyer, D. The counselor as consultant: Rationale and procedures. *Elementary School Guidance and Counseling*, 1968, *2*, 187–194.

Faust, V. *The counselor-consultant in the elementary school.* Boston: Houghton Mifflin Co., 1968.

Feldhusen, J. F., Thurston, J. R., & Benning, J. J. Classroom behavior intelligence and achievement. *Journal of Experimental Education*, 1967, *36*, 82–87.

Glasser, W. *Schools without failure*. New York: Harper & Row, 1969.

Homme, L. E., Csanyi, A. P., Gonzales, M. A., & Roch, J. R. *How to use contingency contracting in the classroom*. Champaign: Research Press, 1969.

McGehearty, L. The case for consultation. *Personnel and Guidance Journal*, 1968, *47*, 257–262.

Missildine, W. H. *Your inner child of the past*. New York: Simon & Schuster, 1963.

Poppen, W. A., & Thompson, C. L. The effects of grade contracts on student performance. *Journal of Educational Research* (in press).

Quay, H. C., Werry, J. S., McQueen, M., & Sprague, R. L. Remediation of the conduct problem child in the special class setting. *Exceptional Children*, 1966, *32*, 509–515.

Rogers, C. R. *Freedom to learn: A view of what education might become.* Columbus, Ohio: C. E. Merrill Publishing Co., 1969.

Toews, J. M. The counselor as contingency manager. *Personnel and Guidance Journal*, 1969, *48*, 127–133.

Thompson, C. L. Counseling elementary school students: Techniques and proposals. *Elementary School Guidance and Counseling*, 1970, *4*, 164–171.

Warters, J. *Techniques of Counseling* (2nd ed.). New York: McGraw-Hill, 1964.

Weinberg, C. Sociological explorations for student problems. *Personnel and Guidance Journal*, 1968, *46*, 852–857.

Wrenn, C. G. *The counselor in a changing world*. Washington, D.C.: American Personnel and Guidance Association, 1962.

THE UTILITY OF BEHAVIOR CONTRACTS AND BEHAVIOR PROCLAMATIONS WITH ADVANTAGED SENIOR HIGH SCHOOL STUDENTS

ROBERT L. WILLIAMS AND JAMES D. LONG

RICHARD W. YOAKLEY

Summary: The relative efficiency of behavioral contracts and behavioral proclamations was empirically appraised in a parochial high school setting. Subjects were a select group of academically oriented seniors studying Problems in Democracy. The study consisted of an intra-subject replication design with eight phases aimed at determining the controlling influences of the experimental conditions for increasing appropriate student behavior. Line graphs and percentage tables were employed to analyze observational data. Results supported the position that students attain higher rates of appropriate behavior when given the opportunity to assist in classroom management. Both behavioral proclamations and contracts proved superior to the standard classroom procedures of the baselines.

Data continue to accumulate supporting the efficacy of contingency management approaches in controlling classroom behavioral problems. Homme (1966), the first researcher to use the term "contingency contract," used written contracts with adolescents who were potential dropouts to specify how existing reinforcers could be earned by completing academic assignments. Cantrell, Cantrell, Huddleston, & Wooldridge (1969) successfully used individual written contracts in managing school problems ranging from hyperagressivity, stealing, and underachievement to school phobia. Parents and/or teachers administered the reinforcers (i.e., outdoor time, money, driving privileges) contingent upon the completion of designated performances. Anandam & Williams (1971) found behavior contracts useful in helping eighth-grade culturally disadvantaged students attain higher rates of study, appropriate social behaviors, and better grades. Keirsey (1969) found that contracts successfully reduced (75-90%) chronic behavior problems. One researcher (Sapp, 1971) compared the effects of contracting and proclamations in a predominately black inner-city school. He demonstrated that levels of specified appropriate behaviors could be increased and maintained equally well with either a behavior proclamation or behavior contract.

As indicated by Sapp's (1970) research, behavior management plans can generally be placed into two categories—contracts and proclamations. If the classroom teacher formulates the classroom management procedures, controls all the contingencies, and imposes the plan without the endorsement of the

JOURNAL OF SCHOOL PSYCHOLOGY, 1972, Vol. 10, pp. 329-338.

students, then the plan is called a behavior proclamation. Token economies are based usually on proclamation. On the other hand, a behavior contract is a plan drawn up jointly by the teacher and students (subject to ratification or rejection by either party) spelling out the responsibilities of each party, enumerating the reinforcers, and indicating the means by which one party will reinforce the other contingent upon requisite performances. In addition, most recent behavior management plans are based on the Premack principle (Premack, 1959). The Premack principle, simply stated, means that student behaviors can be shaped by making what the students prefer (e.g., recess) contingent upon performing less preferred activities (e.g., an academic assignment).

Most contingency management plans, both contracts and proclamations, have been applied to rather serious problem situations. The present study investigated whether such plans would be effective with advantaged middle-class students who were initially emitting high rates of appropriate behavior. Specifically, the present study was designed to answer the following questions: Will both a behavior contract and behavior proclamation produce a higher level of appropriate behavior than baseline conditions? Which will be more effective in facilitating appropriate behavior, a behavior contract or a behavior proclamation.

METHOD

Setting, Subjects, and Teacher

Setting. The study was conducted at a parochial high school (grades 9-12) in Knoxville, Tennessee, which has an enrollment of 275 students from predominately middle-class backgrounds. The students gave every indication of being highly academically oriented. Over 95% of the school's graduates have attended college.

Subjects. The class selected for the present study was a senior class of 16 students studying Problems in Democracy. All of the 16 students participated in all phases of the study, but only four target Ss were observed for changes in specified behaviors. Although the targets would have been considered ideal students in many schools, they were selected as targets because the teacher deemed them to be the most disruptive students in her class. It was hypothesized that if the behavior of these privileged, though somewhat disruptive, students could be changed, that generalizations could be made to students in similar middle-class settings.

Teacher. The teacher, age 24, volunteered to participate in the study because of her interest in behavior modification research. She had completed one year of teaching and was near completion of a master's degree in social studies.

Observation Procedures

Observer training. Ten graduate students from the Department of Educational Psychology and Guidance at the University of Tennessee served as observers. One group of five observers was trained at the beginning of the study and the other midway through the study. Both groups received identical training in the use of a ten-second time interval assessment procedure.

The training procedure for target student observers consisted of their viewing video tapes of simulated classroom situations, making a judgment every ten seconds as to the behavior being emitted by the target student on tape, and at the end of four-minute observational periods comparing their ratings, interval by interval, with those of the trainer. All observers achieved an agreement of 85% or better with the trainer on four, four-minute time segments during a two-hour training session. An agreement occurred when the trainer and observer recorded the same behavior for the same interval. The teacher observers received similar training to those of target student observers except for viewing and recording teacher behaviors.

Student behaviors. Each target was observed twice for four minutes during the 55-minute class period under study. Observation of targets was systematically varied to ensure that no target was observed at the same time or in the same sequence on a day-to-day basis.

The behaviors of the students were classified into two main categories—appropriate and inappropriate. Appropriate behaviors included Task Relevant (Tr) behaviors and Appropriate Social Interaction (S). A behavior was considered Task Relevant if it was consistent with the classroom learning activity, e.g., hand raising to get teacher's attention, writing when directed to do so, looking at another student who was participating in the lesson. An S behavior was recorded for responses such as laughing, playing games, talking, and the like, when these behaviors were not forbidden by the teacher and when the students had not been instructed to do otherwise.

Inappropriate behaviors included two subdivisions—Time Off Task (To) and four classes of disruptive behaviors. Time Off Task was recorded when a target was engaged in a nonlesson activity that was nondisruptive in nature. For example, gazing out the window and similar nonacademic responses were recorded as To. The classes of disruptive behaviors included Motor Behaviors (M), Noise Making (N), Verbalization (V), and Aggressions (A). In rating two or more disruptive behaviors which occurred simultaneously, priority was given in the following order: A, V, N, M. For instance, a Motor Behavior which involved disruptive noise was recorded as N. In addition, the inappropriate component was recorded any time an appropriate and inappropriate behavior occurred simultaneously.

Teacher behaviors. Assessment of teacher behaviors was undertaken to evaluate whether the teacher's behavior was remaining constant throughout the study or was confounding the influence of the experimental variables. No attempt was made to manipulate teacher responses. The only requirement for the teacher was that she be able to implement the proclamation and contract phases of the study.

Five major categories were established for teacher behavior: Attending to Appropriate Student Behaviors, Attending to Inappropriate Student Behaviors, Routine Tasks, Socializing, and Time Out. Attending to Appropriate Student Behaviors included Verbal Approval, Nonverbal Approval, Instruction, and Neutral Attention to Appropriate Student Behaviors. Verbal Disapproval, Facial Disapproval, and Corporal Punishment were ratings subsumed under Attending to Inappropriate Student Behaviors.

Experimental Sequence

The study consisted of eight phases $(A_1, B_1, A_2, C_1, A_3, B_2, A_4, C_2)$. The first phase (A_1) was the establishment of a baseline for student and teacher behaviors against which subsequent measurements could be compared. Phase 2 (B_1) involved the implementation of the behavior contract. The contract was withdrawn and baseline re-established in phase 3 (A_2). The fourth phase (C_1) consisted of the implementation of a behavior proclamation plan. The final four phases entailed repeating the sequence of the first four phases to ascertain if observed changes were in fact the result of controlled experimental variables.

Baseline. Observational data were obtained during baseline to show the frequency of designated teacher and student behaviors under standard classroom procedures. The teacher was asked to conduct class according to her regular routine. Thus, the baseline provided a reference point for measuring the effect of the experimental treatments.

Contract management plan. In the last week of the initial baseline (A_1), students were told that soon they would be given the opportunity to assist in planning the management of classroom activities. At that time the students responded to a survey which permitted them to provide input for the formulation of a contract. The students wrote answers to three questions: (a) What behaviors do you consider appropriate in the classroom setting? (b) What behaviors would you not permit in the classroom setting? (c) If you had free time during the class period—time in which you could do what you wanted within the limits of school rules and reason—what activities would you choose?

The following week a tentative contract was drafted and presented to the students for their evaluation. The tentative draft contained many of the students' recommendations. Nonetheless, a few students had expressed a desire for free-time activities not in keeping with school policy. For example, several students wanted to go to their cars to smoke during free time. This type of suggestion was not incorporated into the contract. All of the students, however, signed the contract and it was immediately implemented. Likewise, the teacher signed each pupil's contract (both parties retaining a copy) and each party was then obligated to abide by its terms.

The contract was composed of six sections. Section I (Being Prepared for Class) included such behaviors as being on time to class, bringing appropriate books to class, and bringing appropriate materials to class. Points were awarded each day for these behaviors. The students, for example, received one point for being on time to class. A pupil was considered late if he arrived after the classroom door was closed. Behaviors such as being late had previously interfered with classroom learning (Task Relevant Behavior). Section II (Working in Class) clarified how students could earn points for engaging in lesson activities. The third section specified the negative behaviors for which the students would be penalized. The negative behaviors included those behaviors which the teacher, as well as many students, wanted decreased in frequency. The assignment of grades was explained in Section IV. The privileges to be gained by accumulating a requisite number of points was specified in the fifth section of the contract. All privileges (e.g., reading magazines, reading books, drawing, listening to the radio with ear plugs) were adopted from student recommendations. The final section of the contract specified the daily procedures and contained the pledge of both parties (teacher and students) to abide by the terms of the agreement. Minor changes (e.g., additional free-time activities) were made when the contract was re-introduced later (B_2) in the study.

The teacher used a daily chart to record points. Daily record keeping required only a few minutes of teacher time. Points were easily recorded while class was in progress. The chart provided an efficient means of identifying students who were entitled to free time. In addition, the chart was used to compute weekly grades

Proclamation management plan. During the initial proclamation plan (C_1) and the reimplementation of the plan (C_2), the teacher was the sole contingency manager. That is, the teacher developed the plan, controlled all the consequences for student behaviors, and expected the students to comply with her ideas. The teacher informed the students on the first day of the proclamation that the classroom would be run differently for the next few weeks. Essentially, the students were required to function under the same contingencies spelled out earlier in the contract phase. However, the students were in no way asked to contribute to the plan nor were they asked for an endorsement. The teacher alone specified what was considered appropriate and inappropriate, enumerated the consequences for different behaviors, and dispensed rewards (i.e., grades, free time) in accordance with her ideas. The students continued to earn free time and grades contingent upon earning a required number of points.

RESULTS

Figure 1 represents the mean percentage of Appropriate Behavior, Time Off Task, and Disruptive Behavior for all targets under every condition of the study. Only weekly averges were plotted because of the marked fluctuation in student behaviors from day to day. The daily fluctuations may have resulted in part from divergence in lesson activities and uncontrolled variables outside the classroom. In the initial baseline (A), group data revealed that targets emitted very high rates of appropriate behavior (an average of 77% for both weeks combined). The introduction of the first behavioral contract facilitated even higher frequencies of desired behavior (87.5%). It is obvious that each time an experimental condition was in effect that an increment in appropriate behavior occurred (see Figure 1). It should be noted, however, that measures of appropriate behavior were lower on each return to baseline. Also, with the exception of the final proclamation, the treatments decreased in potency over the course of the study. Since the study began in October and terminated in March, a considerable degree of change may have occurred as a result of these students approaching the end of their high school careers.

69

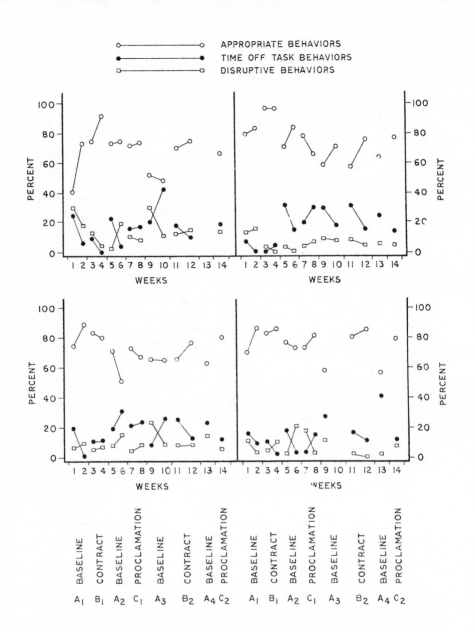

Figure 1. Weekly mean frequency for designated student behaviors

Mean percentages of Inappropriate Behaviors (Time Off Task and Disruptive Behaviors) reached a peak during the ninth and tenth weeks of the study. Even at their worst, though, the students never presented any serious disciplinary problems for the teacher. In regard to disruptive behavior, the researchers had anticipated that some physically aggressive behavior would be

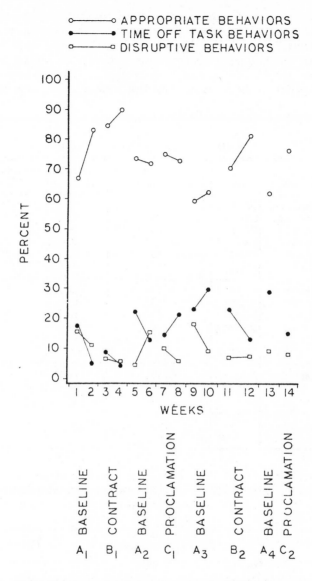

Figure 2. Weekly frequency of designated behaviors for individual target students

evidenced among students or against objects (e.g., school furniture). Thus, an observational category was established for this type of behavior. During the experiment over ten thousand student responses were recorded. Not a single aggressive response was observed!

Data for individual targets are presented in Figure 2. Experimental conditions did not have the same effect on all subjects. For example, Subject 4 emitted higher rates of appropriate behavior every time a contract (B_1 and

B_2) or proclamation (C_1 and C_2) was introduced, but Subject 2 emitted an equal amount of appropriate behavior under the baseline and proclamation phases. Table 1, nevertheless, illustrates the superiority of the experimental conditions. The two contracts combined produced the greatest amount of appropriate student behavior with every subject. The proclamations also proved superior to the standard classroom procedures for three of the four subjects.

Table 1
Student Behaviors for Combined Phases

Percentage	Targets	Baselines (A_1, A_2, A_3, & A_4)	Contracts (B_1 & B_2)	Proclamations (C_1 & C_2)
Percentage of	Subject 1	61	80	71
Appropriate	Subject 2	74	83	74
Student	Subject 3	69	78	74
Behavior	Subject 4	71	85	79
(Tr & S)	All Subjects	69	82	75
Percentage of	Subject 1	21	10	18
Time Off	Subject 2	17	13	21
Task	Subject 3	19	15	20
(To)	Subject 4	19	11	10
	All Subjects	19	12	17
Percentage of	Subject 1	18	10	11
Disruptive	Subject 2	9	4	5
Behaviors	Subject 3	12	7	6
(M, N, V, & A)	Subject 4	10	4	11
	All Subjects	12	6	8

Teacher behavior remained fairly stable from day-to-day throughout the study. Consequently, it can be concluded that changes in the target students' behaviors were due to the experimental treatments rather than to changes in the teacher's behavior.

DISCUSSION

Since most classroom behavior modification studies have been done with students presenting serious social or academic problems, the question has frequently arisen as to the effectiveness of such procedures with students who are already emitting high rates of appropriate behavior. Some teachers contend that when students are achievement oriented and when the content of a class is relevant, neither a behavior proclamation nor a contract increases the proficiency of classroom operations.

The present study demonstrated that both a proclamation and contract will increase the level of appropriate behavior among high-achieving, advan-

.aged students. The increase in appropriate behavior will undoubtedly be less than that required in many studies of behavioral problem students. For example, the comparative levels of appropriate behaviors for the baseline and contracting phases in the present study were 69% and 82%, respectively. It is obvious that there is less room for improvement when the baseline of appropriate behavior is 70% than when it is 25%. Upon implementation of a behavior contract system, the teacher of a disruptive, disadvantaged class may find that the level of appropriate behavior increases from 25 to 75%. In this case, most teachers would probably consider the implementation of a behavior contract system worth their effort. In contrast, if the level of appropriate behavior is already about 70%, is it worthwhile to implement a behavior contract system to increase appropriate behavior by 10 percentage points? Undoubtedly teachers will provide different answers to this question.

A second purpose of the study was to appraise the relative potency of a behavior contract and a behavior proclamation in facilitating appropriate behavior. Much is being written about the necessity of involving students in the formulation of classroom procedures. The behavior contracting system maximizes student involvement, i.e., students participate in the identification of appropriate classroom behaviors, inappropriate behaviors, and rewards for appropriate behaviors. They also have the option of ratifying or rejecting such a system. The behavior contracting system seemed to be particularly appropriate for a class which was studying problems in a democracy. In contrast, under a proclamation the teacher spells out and imposes the contingencies on the class. The present study indicates that for advantaged, high-achieving students the level of appropriate behavior is slightly higher (7 percentage points) under a contract than under a proclamation. One possible reason for the similarity in results under these two conditions is that the proclamation incorporated many of the same contingencies as were in effect under the contract. When contingencies are clearly delineated and basically acceptable to students, formal participation in the formulation and ratification of such contingencies may not be vitally important. On the other hand, a proclamation would probably be much less effective if the contingencies were unclear or unacceptable to students. One strong point of contracting is that it does maximize the likelihood of clarity and acceptability of contingencies to the students who will operate under the system.

REFERENCES

Anandam, K., & Williams, R. L. A model for consultation with classroom teachers on behavior management. *School Counselor*, 1971, *18*, 233-259.

Cantrell, R. P., Cantrell, M. L., Huddleston, C. M., & Wooldridge, R. L. Contingency contracting with school problems. *Journal of Applied Behavior Analysis*, 1969, *2*, 215-220.

Homme, L. Human motivation and the environment. In N. Haring and R. Whelan (Eds.), *The learning environment: Relationship to behavior modification and implications for special education*. Lawrence: University of Kansas Press, 1966.

Keirsey, D. W. Systematic exclusion: Eliminating chronic classroom disruptions. In J. D. Krumboltz and C. E. Thoreson (Eds.), *Behavioral counseling: Cases and techniques*. New York: Holt, Rinehart, and Winston, 1969.

Premack, D. Toward empirical behavioral laws. I. Positive reinforcement. *Psychological Review*, 1959, *66*, 219-233.

Sapp, G. L. The application of contingency management systems to the classroom behavior of Negro adolescents. Paper presented at the meeting of the American Personnel and Guidance Association, Atlantic City, April, 1971.

CONTINGENCY COUNSELING BY SCHOOL PERSONNEL: AN ECONOMICAL MODEL OF INTERVENTION[1]

W. Scott MacDonald, Ronald Gallimore, and Gwen MacDonald

Several recent demonstrations have indicated that the involvement of significant persons in the lives of the "targets" of intervention often enhance the success of contingency management programs (Tharp and Wetzel, 1969; Martin, Burkholder, Rosenthal, Tharp, and Thorne, 1968). Such approaches persuade "natural mediators" (Tharp and Wetzel, 1969; Zeilberger, Sampen, and Sloane, 1968), such as parents, spouses, and friends to distribute the resources they control, contingent on the target performing criterion behaviors. Further, by using non-Ph.D. personnel for direct contacts with targets and mediators, Tharp and Wetzel (1969) and Zeilberger et al. (1968) have evolved an extra-institutional, community-based intervention model that is both effective and economical. Both Tharp and Wetzel, and Martin et al. (1968) employed as their "consultants" specially trained personnel (called "behavior analysts") not connected officially with schools or other agencies; the behavior analysts monitored and counseled the mediators to insure correct dispensing of the reinforcers to the targets. Phillips (1968) demonstrated the effectiveness of naturally occuring reinforcers such as TV privileges, riding bicycles, etc., on modifying a variety of behaviors with predelinquent boys.

The present studies examined the feasibility of utilizing currently available school personnel as the behavior analysts in an attendance-counseling program following the model outlined by Tharp and Wetzel. Implementation depended on the cooperation of personnel who could identify and contact truants and who were familiar enough with the truants to know what could serve as meaningful reinforcers for them, as well as who controlled access to reinforcers for the truants.

STUDY 1

Subjects

Six students were identified as chronic non-attenders by a school counselor. Although the students were enrolled in a "special motivation class", their truancy from school had increased over the school year. The students were ninth graders and, before collection of baseline data, had a 30% average attendance record. During

[1]This research was partially supported by an NIMH grant to the Bernice Pauahi Bishop Museum, Honolulu; support for data analysis and manuscript preparation was provided by the Social Science Research Institute, University of Hawaii. Appreciation is due Edward Kubany and Roland Tharp for critical reading of the manuscript, and to Mrs. Helen Takauchi for her assistance in editing and preparing the manuscript.

JOURNAL OF APPLIED BEHAVIOR ANALYSIS, 1970, Vol. 3, pp. 175-182.

75

the previous year, three of them had quit school early in spring, returning in the fall but continuing to attend irregularly.

Staff Selection and Training

The school system hired a local parent to serve as liaison between the school and residents. This person, a young mother with limited college experience in one university extention course, was released part-time to serve as an Attendance Counselor. Since time was limited, the counselor was provided a brief introduction to the value of attendance counseling based on securing the cooperation of significant persons (mediators) in a student's (target's) life. Approximately 90 min was spent informally discussing how to make "deals" with mediators; a "deal" was an agreement on the part of a mediator to provide a target, a reinforcer contingent on school attendance according to a prearranged schedule. In effect, a "deal" was a contract between a mediator and a target (Tharp and Wetzel, 1969; Martin *et al.*, 1968). "Deal" was discovered by the counselor to be a term that most mediators found agreeably descriptive of the contingencies they placed on the targets. In this particular population, mostly indigenous Hawaiian, a "deal" with a youngster was apparently acceptable, and could be distinguished from a "bribe", which was unacceptable.

The Attendance Counselor accompanied one of the experimenters (the senior author) on a visit with the parents of a student (not one of the six in the present study) who was truant; during this visit the counselor was able to witness the establishment of a "deal". After that one experience, consultations by the experimenters were limited to weekly sessions with the counselor, sometimes conducted by telephone. Throughout the course of the study, repeated emphasis was placed on accurate recording of student attendance, number of contacts, and details of each "deal".

Procedure and Conditions

Attendance data. The school registrar, as a school routine, sent attendance cards to all homeroom teachers in the morning of each school day. The homeroom period, the first 15 min of each day, was the time during which attendance was taken by teachers, recording absences on the attendance cards. The cards were then returned to the school office. The registrar compiled these results and developed a daily Attendance Sheet sent to each faculty member so all teachers had access to information about students who were absent, and those who were supposed to be in class. Irregularities were brought to the registrar's attention; for example, students who came to school after homeroom period appeared on the next day's Attendance Sheet as "tardy". Thus, the absences of the students in the special motivation class were noted by the special motivation teacher and recorded by the registrar. Corrections in the attendance records (tardies and excused illness) were made by these same two persons. The attendance figures reported in this study were taken directly from the daily Attendance Sheet after the experimental period ended. While the registrar did not know of the study, the special motivation teacher did know that the Attendance Counselor was working with some of his students (though the counselor had not contacted the teacher) and did have the opportunity to introduce biased information into the study once the project was identified. In the contacts the senior experimenter had with him, he showed no inclination to bias the attendance count. He apparently was not aware which six of his students were involved.

Procedure. After the brief training sessions, the Attendance Counselor identified six subjects whose names were provided by the school counselor and began selecting the mediators. Mediator candidates for each boy were suggested by teachers, the regular school counselor, and other school personnel whom the Attendance Counselor believed knew something about the target's out-of-school life. Potential mediators were initially contacted in person to establish if they would be suitable. In three cases this initial contact provided information about more likely mediators and the person originally contacted was not involved further. From these contacts, the counselor determined the reinforcers that could be made contingent on attendance. Two mothers, a father, a grandmother, the mother of a girl friend, and a pool-hall proprietor served as mediators.

In most cases, the Attendance Counselor needed no assistance in selecting the reinforcers or arranging a suitable "deal". In one case she sought clearance with school officials to use a target's access to a pool hall, and in another case she discussed with the experimenter the feasibility of using the student's fancy clothing because it seemed to involve rather unusual procedures. In other cases, money and privileges on weekends served as reinforcers. In two cases, the Attendance Counselor and mediator had to alter the reinforcer from after-school privileges to weekend privileges because the former were not really controlled by the mediator. One "deal" used time with a girl friend as a reinforcer. The target, as far as could be determined, did not consider her part in the negotiation disruptive or uncomplementary to the relationship.

After the "deals" were negotiated, the Attendance Counselor made subsequent contacts with mediators in person, by telephone, or by messenger as seemed required to maintain the "deals". The Attendance Counselor maintained the "deals" for seven weeks. Then, without notice, she was called away from the situation, and provided no supervision of the "deals" for two weeks. She returned for two weeks, during which time she attempted to reestablish the original deals. There was a baseline (attendance data before the start of the project), a treatment period (the seven weeks of contingency counseling), a reversal (absence of the counselor), and reinstitution of the deals (two weeks of contingency counseling).

RESULTS AND DECISION

Figure 1 presents the average weekly attendance for the six students in the attendance counseling program. Baseline data were based on those weeks occurring before the first contacts were obtained from the identical source (daily Attendance Sheets).

The increase in average weekly attendance by the students in the seventh week appears to be a direct result of the "deals" established the preceding week. The effect of the attendance counseling seemed to continue over the next seven weeks. This interpretation is consistent with an impressionistic report by the Attendance Counselor that abrupt improvement in average attendance followed the initial "deals" and subsequent refinements yielded continued attendance.

Examination of the data for individuals illustrates details of the effects of the "deals" otherwise obscured by grouping. Figure 2 shows the attendance curves of two boys whose

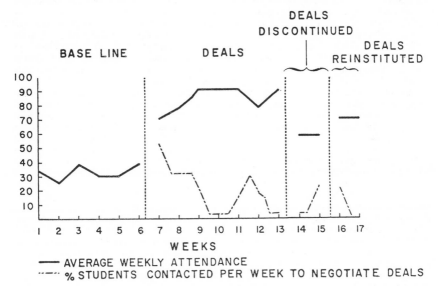

Fig. 1. A record of weekly average attendance for six intermediate school students who participated in attendance counseling.

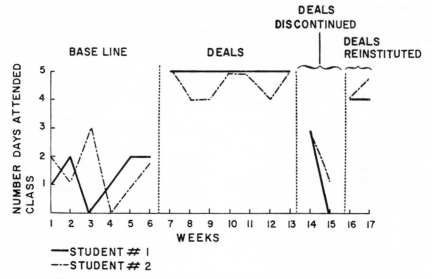

Fig. 2. A record of weekly attendance for two intermediate school students who participated in attendance counseling: Pattern 1.

attendance was clearly dependent on the continued supervision of the deals. After an initial rise in attendance (week seven) and maintained good attendance (weeks 8 to 12), their weekly average dropped when the counselor terminated contacts. One boy ran away from home, and the other got into an altercation with his father, after which the boy went into hiding. When the counselor returned, lengthy negotiations began, and the "deals" were reinstituted with the clearly demonstrated effects. Thus, in these two cases, the need for ongoing management of the deals was demonstrated.

Figure 3 presents the attendance of two boys who did not show the "reversal" effect. The attendance curves seem to indicate that once "deals" have been established, stable school attending resulted. When the Attendance Counselor absented herself, attendance and access to reinforcers continued unabated. The counselor was unable to determine for these two cases whether the mediators encouraged continuance of the "deals" (in one case, weekend nights out; in the other, access to girl friend); or whether the attendance behavior continued in the absence of supervision. From

the behavior of the two boys, the Attendance Counselor concluded that the establishment of the contingencies had become a semiautonomous "deal". She concluded that supervision of the "deals" had become perfunctory and the negotiation of the original "deal" seemed to have been all that was necessary for stable school attendance.

Figure 4 shows the attendance curves of two boys whose contingency attendance performances was rather irregular. These two boys were dropped by the school in the spring of the previous year, and were already considered "lost" for the semester when they were picked up by the Attendance Counselor. One (Case 6) responded somewhat to the deal when it was arranged with a grandmother to control his access to money contingent on school behavior; however, it became evident he had a second source, and his mother had to be persuaded to become a part of the "deal" before full control of his reinforcer could be established. This was established at week nine, and the counselor maintained supervision of the mediators in at least two contacts per week (by telephone and face-to-face) until reversal. This close contact seemed essential to gain any de-

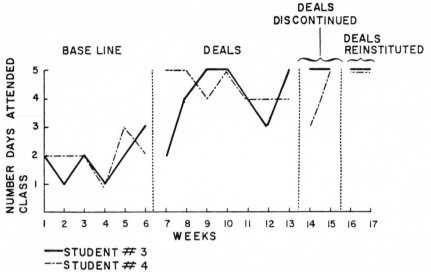

Fig. 3. A record of weekly attendance for two intermediate school students who participated in attendance counseling: Pattern 2.

gree of compliance with the conditions of the "deal" by both mediators. The other case (Case 5) was begun with only minimal change in attendance for the first weeks. The deal was to permit the boy to use the pool hall if he attended school; at first he did not attend school

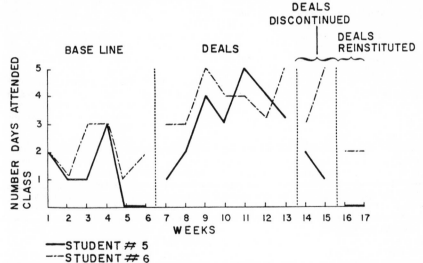

Fig. 4. A record of weekly attendance for two intermediate school students who participated in attendance counseling: Pattern 3.

but still showed up for pool games. The Attendance Counselor emphasized to the proprietor the importance to the boy's future of his attending school and the importance of pool in the "deal". Thereafter, the boy attended more regularly (weeks 9 to 12).

During reversal for Cases 5 and 6, both "deals" broke down and in one case (Case 5) the boy got into trouble in the pool hall and ran away from home and could not be located for the rest of the school year. In the other (Case 6), the boy obtained a supply of money from his mother the last day of the reversal and showed up at school only irregularly thereafter. In these two "irregular" cases, the Attendance Counselor was unable to reinstitute the deals; in one case because the boy disappeared and in the other because the mother of the boy could not be contacted and apparently did not dispense the reinforcer contingent on his attendance behavior.

The data suggested that even with serious truants, relatively untrained personnel can establish and supervise relationships and resulting advantages accruing from involvement of "natural mediators". The nature of the involvement of the Attendance Counselor varied considerably, from simply getting the "deal" established on the one hand to regular and continued support on the other. It appeared to be evident to the counselor which "deals" needed constant supervision, and which could be supported with token contacts or phone calls. The study suggested that relatively untrained school personnel can act in the capacity of managing large numbers of natural mediators. To test the model with a larger population of truants, a second study was made.

STUDY 2

Subjects

Thirty-five students were identified as chronic nonattenders by a school counselor in the same school district as those subjects in Study 1. Fifteen of the students were high school seniors; the remaining 20 were tenth graders. The overall average weekly attendance for the 35 students in the semester preceding the study was about 50%.

Staff Selection and Training

Two school counselors and the registrar volunteered to serve, in addition to their other duties, as counselors for the study. No effort was made to provide the three participants with a general knowledge of reinforcement principles or behavior modification techniques. One counselor and the registrar were given a 2-hr lecture on contingency management, selection of natural mediators, identification of reinforcers, and negotiation of "deals". They were called Contingency Counselors. The second counselor was engaged in a 2-hr discussion of techniques of establishing rapport, contacting truants, and so forth. She was called a Contact Counselor. All three were provided a system of recording contacts between counselor and target, and in the case of the Contingency Counselors, between counselor and mediators.

Procedure and Conditions

Attendance data. The school registrar, one of the participating Contingency Counselors routinely supervised a system of recording attendance cards similar to the system described in Study 1. The registrar had student help to make the actual transfer of information from the daily cards turned in by homeroom teachers to the daily Attendance Sheet. She had earlier in the year selected and trained students to carry out the clerical work. After training for participation in the study, her involvement in record keeping was supervisory. The attendance figures reported here were taken by the registrar's chief assistant (a student without knowledge of the study) directly from the attendance cards officially used to determine school attendance.

Procedure. The Contingency Counselors contacted targets at school, by telephone, or by visits to local areas and establishments known to be frequented by truants. From initial contacts, the Contingency Counselors determined the reinforcers, and who might serve as mediators. Time with peers was the most frequently employed reinforcers established, though as in the first study, various other reinforcers were used. For example, access to family car was used in one case, weekly movies in an additional four. In about half the cases, parents served as mediators; in four cases the counselors themselves were mediators. In others, uncles, friends (adults), and in the case of a married student, a spouse, served as mediators. While the counselors usually negotiated the "deals" between mediator and target in

80

face-to-face meetings, there were some "deals" arranged solely by a target and mediator, though the counselor set the conditions before negotiations and closely supervised the management of all deals. In cases in which the counselors served as mediators, the parents gave the counselors money for theater tickets, and because they worked late and left home early in the morning, could not supervise school attendance. In these cases, the Attendance Counselors contacted the targets, arranged a means by which teachers could report daily attendance, and required the girls to check in the Contingency Counselor's office each day to ensure compliance.

The Contact Counselor followed similar procedures, though she did not establish "deals". Rather she attempted to impress the students that, school was vocationally important, failure to finish school reflected unfavorably on their parents, and tried to work out the personal problems considered to be the root of nonattendance.

RESULTS AND DISCUSSION

Figure 5 shows the average weekly attendance of the 20 students in the Contingency

Counseling condition. The improvement in their attendance occurred in two increments: the first after initial contacts, and the second after the Contingency Counselors refined their deals and made adjustments where necessary. While individual variability was evident in school attending behavior in Contingency Counseling, as it was in Study One, the group curve reflects the general impact of the experimental procedures on the attending behavior of students.

Figure 6 shows the average weekly attendance of the 15 students in the Contact Counseling condition. These 15 students appear to have attended less regularly rather than improving in attendance during the experimental period (weeks 7 to 17). The argument that mere contact with targets and mediators was responsible for the increased attendance obtained by the Contingency Counselors is contradicted by the apparent inability of the Contact Counselor to achieve an increase over baseline. Indeed, over the course of the study, the Contact Counselor made nearly three times as many contacts (X = 5.9) per student as the Contingency Counselors (X = 1.9) did in their negotiation of deals; in spite of her efforts, the data suggest a decrease in attendance

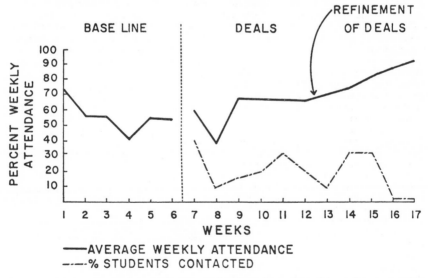

Fig. 5. A record of weekly attendance for 20 high school students who participated in contingency counseling

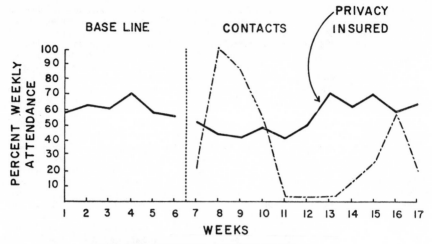

BASE LINE   CONTACTS   PRIVACY INSURED

AVERAGE WEEKLY ATTENDANCE
% STUDENTS CONTACTED PER WEEK

Fig. 6. A record of weekly attendance for 15 high school students who participated in contact counseling.

over the 11-week experimental period. The Contact Counselor attributed her negative results to peer ridicule directed toward students required to visit a counselor; when the method of making contact was altered to insure privacy (after the twelfth week), the Contact Counselor succeeded in promoting by the end of the semester an average attendance slightly below baseline. This failure by the Contact Counselor to achieve improved attendance could be attributed to individual ability rather than technique. However, it is suggestive that Contingency Counseling conducted by two "lay" counselors as well as one with experience was more effective than the more traditional techniques where "individual style" may be an important factor in success.

The data from both studies suggest that personnel functioning in roles widely accepted in public schools can learn with relatively brief training to capitalize on the advantages that accrue from the involvement of "natural mediators". However, it should be noted that the teachers of the targets involved in the Contingency and Reversal groups reported no changes in quality of academic performance in spite of improved attendance; whether school personnel in the present study could have ex-

tended the "deals" to include academic behavior is an open question. Previous work (Tharp and Wetzel, 1969) has shown that "natural mediators" can have a highly positive impact on the school performance of deviant youth referred for special services. Employing school personnel as "natural mediators" to arrange contingency management of student academic performanc as well as compliance with rules deserves investigation.

REFERENCES

Martin, M., Burkholder, R., Rosenthal, T. L., Tharp, R. G., and Thorne, G. Programming behavior change and reintegration into school milieu of extreme adolescent deviates. *Behavior Research and Therapy*, 1968, **6**, 371-384.

Phillips. E. L. Achievement place: token reinforcement procedures in a home-style rehabilitation setting for "pre-delinquent" boys. *Journal of Applied Behavior Analysis*, 1968, 1, 213-224.

Tharp, R. G. and Wetzel, R. J. *Behavior modification in the natural environment.* New York: Academic Press, 1969.

Zeilberger, J., Sampen, S. E., and Sloane, H. N., Jr. Modification of a child's problem behaviors in the home with the mother as therapist. *Journal of Applied Behavior Analysis.* 1968, 1, 35-46.

SECTION THREE

THE ROLE OF TEACHER ATTENTION

Multitudinous studies have demonstrated that social
attention is effective in modifying the responses of young
children. In fact, social attention has been the most
frequently used intervention strategy at that age level.
The simplicity of the attention paradigm is staggering:
children emit behaviors that result in attention and stop
engaging in behaviors which are ignored. Despite its
effectiveness with kindergarten and primary age children,
teacher attention might be quite ineffective with junior
and senior high school students. In the first place, adolescents' behavior may be controlled more directly by internal phenomena than by external events. In the second place,
adolescents may be much more responsive to peer attention than
teacher attention. Both of these possibilities would militate
against the potency of teacher attention with adolescents.
However, the few studies (Atkinson, Davis, and Sanborn, 1972;
Cormier and Wahler, 1971; McAllister, Stachowiak, Baer, and
Conderman, 1969) which have appraised the impact of teacher
attention on adolescent behavior demonstrate that its
effectiveness with junior and senior high school students
closely corresponds to its effect on kindergarten and
elementary students.

A number of secondary questions will evolve from our
examination of the teacher attention research. For instance,
is the amount of attention the most important consideration
in using this strategy to modify adolescents' behavior? As
long as adolescents receive X amount of positive attention,
does it make any difference when and in what manner that
attention is delivered? Cormier and Wahler's study (1971)
suggests that it may make less difference than we had previously thought. Another issue relates to type of teacher
attention. For example, would non-directive attention be as
effective as specific approval? The Atkinson et al. study
addresses itself to this question. A third issue deals with
the effects of contingent teacher approval on non-target
students. Will an adolescent's behavior be affected positively
or adversely by his seeing other students approved for appropriate behavior? Examine Cormier and Wahler's study for some
words of wisdom on this question. A final issue has to do with
the most judicious means for dealing with inappropriate student
responses. Granted that the teacher should consistently attend
to appropriate behavior, but how should he respond to undesirable behavior? Should he ignore it or disapprove of it? The
reader will get some idea of the relative effectiveness of
these two approaches by comparing the findings of the Cormier
and Wahler study and the McAllister et al. study.

THE APPLICATION OF SOCIAL REINFORCEMENT IN SIX
JUNIOR HIGH SCHOOL CLASSROOMS[1]

William H. Cormier   Robert G. Wahler

The effective use of contingent social reinforcement in
the modification of children's behavior in elementary school
classrooms has been demonstrated in a number of studies (Becker,
Madsen, Arnold, and Thomas, 1967; Hall, Lund, and Jackson, 1968;
Madsen, Becker, and Thomas, 1968; Sibley, Abbott, and Cooper,
1969). However, no research has systematically examined these
procedures in the secondary school classroom. In fact, most
investigations that have used the principles of reinforcement
with adolescents have employed tokens or money in changing
their behavior. Also, these studies have been conducted either
in predominately institutionalized settings or with rather
specialized populations (Burchard and Tyler, 1965; Clark,
Lachowicz, and Wolf, 1968; Phillips, 1968; Staats, Minke,
Goodwin, and Landeen, 1967).

Classroom investigations that have applied teacher contingent approval or praise have chosen one or two target
children to receive praise. Two investigators have reported
that their teachers noticed a change in the non-target pupils
(other members of the class) as well as in the overall classroom atmosphere (Hall et al., 1968; Madsen et al., 1968). No
corroborative data were collected to verify these reports.
The degree to which contingent teacher praise might generalize
to non-target pupils warrants investigation.

The few studies that have used non-contingent reinforcement in the natural setting have not been effective in altering
(increasing) the desired behavior (Bushell, Wrobel, and
Michaelis, 1968; Hart, Reynolds, Baer, Brawley, and Harris,
1968; Redd, 1969). However, there is evidence to suggest that
non-contingent (random) social reinforcement may increase the
appropriate behavior of lower class adolescents. Cormier (1969)
found that teachers very infrequently praise lower class
adolescents for appropriate classroom behavior. It may be that
the withholding and presentation of approval alter the motivation for obtaining approval (Eisenberger, 1970). More direct
evidence of the effects of non-contingent praise appeared in a
recent study (McAllister, Stachowiak, Baer, and Conderman, 1969).
The authors assessed the effects of teacher praise and disapproval on two target behaviors (inappropriate talking and
turning around) in a high school English class of 25 students.
Teacher praise was administered after a time period in which
no inappropriate talking occurred and was directed toward the
entire class. Eighty percent of the students in the class were
from lower-class families.

[1]Presented at the annual meeting of the American Education
Research Association, New York City, February, 1971.

The purpose of this study was to examine the effects of teacher contingent and non-contingent (random) praise and/or attention on the classroom behavior of economically disadvantaged adolescents. Other purposes were to ascertain the effects of contingent praise on the non-target members of the classroom, and to explore the length of time (days) necessary to demonstrate significant changes in behavior.

METHOD

Subjects

Setting. The subjects were 150 eighth-grade students enrolled in a junior-senior high school in Knoxville, Tennessee. Over 50 percent of the students in the school came from families with an annual income of less than $3,000. One male and five female teachers volunteered and were paid to participate in the study. All teachers had several years of teaching experience. One class period for each teacher was selected for observation. Each teacher chose his most disruptive class. The eighth-grade courses taught during these class periods were three English, two mathematics, and one health. All class periods were in the morning with the exception of one afternoon mathematics class. The study was conducted during the second semester. All students had the same teacher for the first semester.

Target and Non-Target Students. Each teacher identified three target students in his class as being either disruptive or not motivated to do the assigned work. The three target students and three other members of the class (non-target) were observed daily.

Procedure

Behavioral Categories. After several weeks of observing and recording the most common student behavior for each class, the behaviors were grouped into categories on the basis of similarity. The following three categories of student behavior were rated. Appropriate behaviors consisted of answering questions orally which were lesson oriented, writing assignments or answers to questions when directed to do so by the teacher, reading a book or head oriented toward the book, hand raised in order to get the teacher's attention during a lesson, and following the teacher's instructions. Relevant behaviors were rated only if they did not fit one of the above examples of appropriate behavior. For example, if the student appeared to be oriented or attending to classroom activities, the student's behavior was rated as relevant. Inappropriate behaviors rated were gestures without talking, getting out of seat, walking around, disruptive movements, making disruptive noise with objects, talking or attending to another student during a lesson, blurting out answers without being called on, singing, whistling, laughing, sleeping, and ignoring the teacher's request or questions or doing something different from that which the student or class was directed to do.

Observer Training and Reliability. Six graduate students served as observers. Observer training consisted of a gradual introduction of videotaped illustrations of each behavioral category until each observer became familiar with all of the categories. Also, pairs of observers would rate the classroom behavior of the same student for three to six minutes and then compare their ratings and discuss differences. Reliability checks were made weekly throughout the study. The observers rated student behavior in ten-second time intervals from a video monitor displaying taped classroom sessions. Observers rated these video-taped sessions independently and from these weekly ratings inter-observer reliability was computed. The average reliability between all combinations of observers expressed in terms of a pi-coefficient (Scott, 1955) was .90, with a range of .78 to .97. Classroom reliabilities were also obtained for pairs of observers during the initial phases of the study. The average pi-coefficient was .92, with a range of .78 to .98.

Observation and Rating. For each class three target and three non-target students were observed daily. Except for the target students all members of each class were numbered. A table of random numbers was used daily to select the three non-target students to be observed for each class. Only one behavioral category was rated during a 10 second time interval. If examples of all three categories of behavior occurred during a 10 second interval, observers were instructed to rate according to the following priority: (1) inappropriate, (2) relevant, and (3) appropriate. For example, if a student was writing an assignment (appropriate) and whistling (inappropriate) during a 10 second interval, the observers rated the inappropriate category. Each student (three target and three non-target) was observed daily for a total of 6 minutes. The daily order in which each student was observed was random. Observers rated student behavior on observation sheets which were divided into blocks of 10 second time intervals. Solid-state, cartridge, tape recorders were used as timing devices for each observer. Ten second intervals were recorded and the time sequences announced to the observer the exact intervals. Each recorder had a Y-connector from which two ear plugs were connected. One ear plug had a 3 feet extension and the other a 12 feet. The Y-connector facilitated independent observation for reliability checks using the same tape recorder. The tape recorder eliminated the need for the observer to visually monitor a watch which might distract him from observing and rating.

There was one observer for each class except during times when reliability checks were made. The observers were instructed to sit in back of the classroom in a position that would maximize their observational range without disrupting any normal classroom activity. Also, observers were instructed to avoid all eye contact and interaction with the students and teacher. All observers were in the classroom at least two weeks before the collection of baseline data. Observers were not informed about the sequence of the experimental conditions.

Teacher Training. At the end of the baseline period the teachers read a programmed book on the principles of social reinforcement, which provided them with the rationale for the procedures introduced in their classes (Patterson and Gullion, 1968). If the teacher started the experimental sequence with a control period, this book and the instructions were not presented until the completion of that period. The following instructions were given individually to each teacher:

Contingent Praise and/or Attention (after Madsen et al., 1968)

This phase of the study is designed to increase classroom participation or relevant behaviors through praise and other forms of approval. We are inclined to take relevant classroom behavior for granted and pay attention only to disruptive classroom behaviors. During this phase of our research we would like for you to try something different. The technique that you will use is characterized as "catching the student participating in appropriate classroom behavior" and making a positive comment to the target student. The positive comment or praise is designed to reward the target student for relevant behavior. Give praise, attention, or smile when a target student is doing what is expected during the class period. Specifically, give praise when the target adolescent responds (1) verbally to your questions, directed to him or to the class in general, or to an appropriate classroom recitation, (2) to hand raising in order to recite, (3) to written classroom assignments, and (4) to assigned classroom reading. Start "small" by giving praise and attention at the first signs of appropriate behavior. Watch carefully and when the adolescent participates in terms of any of the four above kinds of behavior, make such comments as "You're doing a fine job, (name)," or "That's good." It is very important during the first few days to catch as many participating behaviors as possible. Even for example if an adolescent has thrown an eraser at you (one minute ago) and is now working or appropriately responding, you should praise the participating behavior. We are assuming that your commendation and praise are important to the student. This is generally the case, but sometimes it takes a while for praise to become effective. Persistence in catching adolescents participating in classroom activity and delivering praise and attention should eventually increase relevant behavior of the target student.

Examples of praise comments are as follows:
I like the way you're doing your work, (name).
That's a very good (paper, answer, report, job), (name).
You're doing fine.
That's very good (if he or she generally gets only a few
    answers correct).
That makes me feel good.

In general, give praise for achievement. Specifically, you can praise for working individually (writing or reading), raising hand when appropriate, responding to questions, paying

attention to directions and following through. Try to use
variety and expression in your comments. Stay away from
sarcasm. Attempt to become spontaneous in your praise and
smile when delivering praise. At first you will probably
get the feeling that you're praising a great deal and it
sounds a little phony to you. This is typical reaction and
it becomes more natural with the passage of time. If comments
sometimes might interfere with the ongoing class activities,
then use facial attention and smiles. Walk around the room
during study time. Praise quietly spoken to a student has
been found effective in combination with some physical sign
of approval. Praise should be given individually to each target student when you catch him participating, and remember to
ignore inappropriate behavior.

Non-Contingent Praise

During this phase of the study you should give non-contingent praise to the entire class. Praise should be presented
according to random intervals of time during the class period.
Also, praise should be given without regard for what student
behavior might be occurring at those times. During the contingent delivery of praise we asked you to give praise when
you "caught" a target student participating in any one of the
appropriate behaviors. The praise was contingent on the student's behavior. Praise during this phase of the study is without regard to what behavior occurred immediately before you
deliver it. Attempt to give praise ten times a class period.
Try to spread your comments over the period. Remember to give
praise to the entire class and to ignore inappropriate behavior.

Ignoring Inappropriate Behavior (Madsen et al., 1968)

During this phase of the study you should learn to ignore
(not attend to) behaviors which interfere with learning or
teaching, unless a student is being hurt by another, in which
case use a punishment which seems appropriate. Learning to
ignore is rather difficult. Most of us pay attention to the
violations. For example, instead of ignoring we often say
such things as: "John, you know you are supposed to be working;"
"Gary, will you stop bothering your neighbors;" "Bert, will you
or can you keep your hands off Bob;" "Mariana, stop running
around and do your work;" "Hank, will you please stop rocking
on your chair."

Behaviors which are to be ignored include motor behaviors
such as getting out of seat, standing up, walking around the
room, moving chairs, or sitting in a contorted manner. Any verbal comment or noise not connected with the assignments should
also be ignored, such as: carrying on conversations with other
members of the class when it is not permitted, answering questions without raising hands or being called on, making remarks
when no questions have been asked, calling your name to get
attention, and extraneous noises such as whistling, laughing
loudly, blowing nose, or coughing. An additional important

group of behaviors to be ignored are those which the student engages in which he is supposed to be doing other things; for example, when the student ignores your instructions you are to ignore him. Any noises made with objects, playing with pencils or other materials should be ignored, as well as taking things from or disturbing another student by turning around and touching or grabbing him.

The reason for this phase of the study is to test the possibility that attention to inappropriate behavior may serve to strengthen the very behavior that the attention is intended to diminish. Inappropriate behavior may be strengthened by paying attention to it even though you may think that you are punishing or decreasing the behavior.

Ignoring inappropriate student behavior should be followed during the phases in which you will deliver contingent and non-contingent phase.

After the instructions were read, the E answered any questions and discussed with each teacher the relationship of the instructions to the principles of social reinforcement. One E instructed all teachers individually by using role playing techniques to demonstrate ignoring inappropriate behavior, contingent praise, and non-contingent praise. All teachers were instructed about the confidential nature of the research. Each teacher was also requested not to discuss with any other teacher what was occurring in his classroom.

Experimental Design

Each teacher began the study with an eight-day baseline phase in which observers rated the classroom behavior of target and non-target students. After the baseline phase, one of the following six conditions occurred: control short (CS), control long (CL), non-contingent short (NCS), non-contingent long (NCL), contingent short (CTS), and contingent long (CTL). The short periods were four school days and the long periods lasted eight days. During the control conditions the teachers were instructed to reinstate the baseline conditions (i.e., attend to inappropriate behavior and infrequently attend to appropriate behavior). Teachers were instructed to ignore inappropriate behavior under contingent and non-contingent conditions. The Es monitored the teacher's behavior for each experimental condition. Es consulted with each teacher individually, almost daily, about any problems that occurred in executing the particular experimental condition. The assignment of teachers and the sequence of the six experimental conditions were random.

RESULTS

To facilitate the analyses between short and long time periods of the experimental and control conditions, ratio scores (RS) were computed for target and non-target students.

89

RS = BE/PT X 100, where BE = the number of behaviors emitted during an experimental or control condition, and baseline, and PT = the possible total number of occasions for observation. Percentages of increase or decrease were selected as dependent variables to indicate the magnitude of emitted behaviors during the experimental conditions. The emitted behavior score (EBS) represented a percentage increase or decrease in the ratio of emitted behaviors during an experimental or a control condition as compared to baseline behaviors. EBS = RS_2 - RS_1, where RS_2 = the ratio of behavior (appropriate, relevant, inappropriate) emitted by a student during an experimental or a control condition, and RS_1 = the ratio of behaviors emitted during baseline. Computation of EBSs had the effect of equating baseline performance to zero.

Target Students. The experimental and control conditions differed significantly for both appropriate (F = 12.76, p < .01) and inappropriate EBSs (F = 22.35, p < .01). Figure 1 shows appropriate, relevant, and inappropriate EBS means of target and non-target students as a function of the six experimental conditions. A post hoc analysis of these means reveals that the contingent short, contingent long, non-contingent long, and non-contingent short conditions produced significantly greater (p < .01) increases in appropriate and decreases in inappropriate behavior than did the control short and control long conditions. No significant differences were obtained between the contingent (L or S) and non-contingent conditions for either appropriate or inappropriate behavior. However, as indicated in Figure 1, the magnitude of changes in appropriate and inappropriate behavior was slightly greater (p < .10) during the contingent long condition than during the non-contingent long. The analysis of variance also indicated a significant effect of the time periods on relevant behavior (F = 12.82, p < .05). A significant contrast of the means for relevant behavior indicated greater mean differences for long periods than for short time periods.

Non-Target Students. The experimental conditions were found significant for appropriate (F = 5.51, p < .05) and inappropriate behaviors (F = 7.99, p < .01) emitted by the three non-target students. The post hoc comparisons of the treatment means yielded significant differences between CTL, CTS, NCL, NCS collectively and the long and short control conditions for both appropriate (p < .05) and inappropriate behavior (p < .01). No significant differences were found between experimental conditions for relevant behavior. Differences between long and short time periods were not significant for any of the behavioral categories.

The magnitude of increments in appropriate and decrements in inappropriate behavior evidenced by target and non-target students were significantly different during both the CTL and CTS conditions (p < .01), with the target students demonstrating the greater changes.

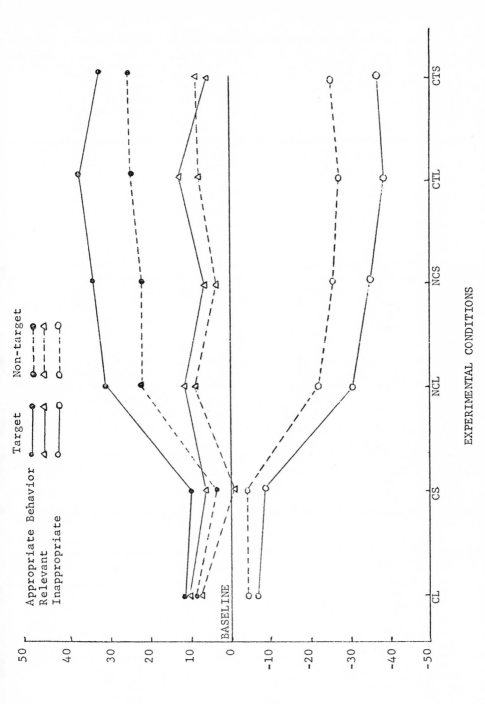

Figure 1. Relevant, inappropriate, and appropriate EBS means of target and non-target Ss as a function of the six experimental conditions.

91

DISCUSSION

The results showed that contingent teacher points and/or attention was effective in controlling the classroom behavior of target adolescents. Teacher praise or attention to desirable behavior in combination with ignoring disruptive behaviors increased appropriate behaviors and concomitantly reduced inappropriate behaviors. These data corroborate results of studies using similar procedures in elementary school settings (Hall et al., 1968; Thomas et al., 1968; Madsen et al., 1968; and Sibley et al., 1969). It appears, then, that the antipathy adolescents ostensibly hold toward adults does not negate the potential effectiveness of teacher approval as a means of modifying their behavior.

Contingent teacher praise or attention administered to target Ss generalized significantly to non-target adolescents. The increases in appropriate behaviors and reduction in inappropriate behaviors that occurred for target Ss was also observed for non-target Ss. The results of this investigation support findings from other experimenters that changes occur in the non-target pupils as a result of praising one or two target children contingently (Hall et al., 1968, Madsen et al., 1968). Also, the data of this study support the hypothesis presented by Kanfer (1965) that vicarious reinforcement provides considerable learning experience in a classroom in which students observe the behavior and reinforcement of others. These results suggest that target students might be models for non-target students. The behaviors of models possibly function as discriminative stimuli in facilitating the expression of similar behaviors by others.

Non-contingent praise increased the percentage of appropriate behavior for target Ss but not to the extent of contingent praise and attention. The same effects also existed for decreases of inappropriate behavior. The impact of non-contingent approval on the target students' behavior is contrary to the finding of other studies that non-contingent praise has minimal effect on students' behavior (Bushell et al., 1968; and Hart et al., 1968). A possible explanation for the potency of non-contingent praise manifested in the present study is that such praise causes the teacher and his class to become associated with positive social stimuli (praise). The frequent (approximately 10 to 14 times per observational period) pairing of praise with the teacher might cause the teacher's presence to elicit something of the same reactions as does praise. This pairing should eventually evoke a positive attitude from the students about the class and/or teacher. We would then assume that students behave more appropriately in classes toward which they feel positively. Staats and Staats (1958) have demonstrated the formation of attitudes to verbal stimuli through classical conditioning. However, it is very difficult to ascertain from the present investigation whether the results of non-contingent praise were a result of a classical conditioning paradigm.

92

Although the results of the non-contingent praise conditions were correlated with significant increases of appropriate behaviors of non-target students, the results were less dramatic than for target students. A possible cause for this effect might be that the average percentage of inappropriate behavior was greater for target students than for non-target students during the baseline conditions. In other classroom studies, the degree of percentage decrease of inappropriate and increase of desired behavior has been attributed to the relatively high or low percentage of inappropriate behavior that occurred during baseline (O'Leary and Becker, 1967; Cormier, 1969). These investigators suggest that the percentage of increase or decrease during treatment is directly related to the percentage of inappropriate or disruptive behavior that occurred during baseline.

REFERENCES

Becker, W. C., Madsen, C. H., J., Arnold, C. R., and Thomas
D. R. The contingent use of teacher attention and praise
in reducing classroom behavior problems. The Journal of
Special Education, 1967, 1, 287-307.

Burchard, J., and Tyler, V., Jr. The modification of delinquent
behavior through operant conditioning. Behaviour Research
and Therapy, 1965, 2, 245-250.

Bushell, D., Jr., Wrobel, P. A., and Michaelis, M. L. Applying
"group" contingencies to the classroom study behavior of
preschool children. Journal of Applied Behavior Analysis,
1968, 1, 55-61.

Clark, M., Lachowicz, J., and Wolf, M. A pilot basic education
program for school dropouts incorporating a token reinforcement system. Behaviour Research and Therapy, 1968,
6, 183-188.

Cormier, W. H. Effects of teacher random and contingent social
reinforcement on the classroom behavior of adolescents.
Unpublished Doctoral dissertation, The University of Tennessee, Knoxville, 1969.

Eisenberger, R. Is there a deprivation-satiation function for
social approval? Psychological Bulletin, 1970, 74, 255-275.

Hall, R. V., Lund, D., and Jackson, D. Effects of teacher
attention on study behavior. Journal of Applied Behavior
Analysis, 1968, 1, 1-12.

Hart, B. M., Reynolds, N. J., Baer, D. M., Brawley, E. R., and
Harris, F. R. Effect of contingent and non-contingent
social reinforcement on the cooperative play of a preschool
child. Journal of Applied Behavior Analysis, 1968, 1, 73-
76.

Kanfer, F. H. Vicarious human reinforcement: A glimpse into the
black box. In L. Krasner and L. P. Ullman (Eds.), Research
in Behavior Modification. New York: Holt, Rinehart, and
Winston, 1965, pp. 244-267.

Madsen, C. H., Jr., Becker, W. C., and Thomas, D. R. Rules,
praise, and ignoring: Elements of elementary classroom
control. Journal of Applied Behavior Analysis, 1968, 1,
139-150.

McAllister, L. W., Stachowiak, J. G., Baer, D. M., and Conderman,
L. The application of operant conditioning techniques in
a secondary school classroom. Journal of Applied Behavior
Analysis, 1969, 2, 277-285.

O'Leary, D. D., and Becker, W. C. Behavior modification in an
adjustment class: A token reinforcement program. Exceptional Children, 1967, 33, 637-642.

Patterson, G. R., and Gullion, M. E. Living with Children.
Champaign, Illinois: Research Press, 1968.

Phillips, E. L. Achievement place: Token reinforcement procedures in a home-style rehabilitation setting for "pre-
delinquent" boys. Journal of Applied Behavior Analysis,
1968, 1, 213-223.

94

Redd, W. H. Effects of mixed reinforcement contingencies on adults' control of children's behavior. *Journal of Applied Behavior Analysis*, 1969, *2*, 249-254.

Scott, W. A. Reliability of content analysis: The case of nominal scale coding. *Public Opinion Quarterly*, 1955, *19*, 231-325.

Sibley, S. A., Abbott, M. S., and Cooper, B. P. Modification of the classroom behavior of a disadvantaged kindergarten boy by social reinforcement and isolation. *Journal of Experimental Child Psychology*, 1969, *7*, 203-219.

Staats, A. W., and Staats, C. K. Attitudes established by classical conditioning. *Journal of Abnormal and Social Psychology*, 1958, *57*, 37-40.

Staats, A. W., Minke, K. A., Goodwin, W., and Landeen, J. Cognitive behavior modification: 'Motivated learning' reading treatment with subprofessional therapy-technicians. *Behaviour Research and Therapy*, 1967, *5*, 283-299.

Donald R. Atkinson

Jerry L. Davis

Marshall P. Sanborn

Behavioral Techniques: Effective with Superior High School Students?

A WIDELY ACCEPTED goal of guidance programs is the development of students' decision-making behavior (Gelatt, 1962; Krumboltz & Thoresen, 1969; Rothney, 1958). Gathering relevant information before making a final decision seems an important aspect of the decision-making process.

A number of studies have attempted to determine if information-seeking behavior is responsive to selected behavioral counseling techniques such as reinforcement counseling and model-reinforcement counseling (Krumboltz & Schroeder, 1965; Krumboltz & Thoresen, 1964; Krumboltz, Varenhorst, & Thoresen, 1967; Meyer, Strowig, & Hosford, 1970). Results of these studies have stimulated further questions. For instance, are the techniques of social-modeling and reinforcement effective with high achieving students who have learned to forego immediate gratification to attain long-range goals? How do these techniques fare when compared to traditional counseling approaches designed to increase information-seeking behavior?

At the University of Wisconsin Research and Guidance Laboratory for Superior Students (hereafter referred to as the Laboratory) problems of identification and guidance of superior high school students have been under investigation for the past 13 years. Arranging personal interviews for high school seniors with persons who are experts in vocational or academic fields of interest is a routine Laboratory procedure. This article reports the results of a Laboratory study that was designed to determine which of three orientation methods—two behavioral and one traditional—was best for preparing youngsters for their interviews. (The traditional method used in this study involved systematic avoidance of reinforcements for student remarks during the orientation sessions. This can only be done by experimenters who exercise considerable restraint. Yet this procedure is practiced by many counselors who attempt to disassociate their own values from counselor-client interaction. If

THE SCHOOL COUNSELOR, 1972, Vol. 19, pp. 254-260.

counsels accept the criterion evaluated in this study as a viable guidance goal, they are no longer in a position to claim exemption from the role of being an active evaluator and reinforcer.)

Method

Subjects

Participants in the study were 29 senior boys and 42 senior girls who visited the Laboratory during fall semester, 1969. When these youngsters were in grade nine they were selected by teachers and counselors in 17 school districts to participate in the Laboratory program. They had taken part in activities of the Laboratory annually since their ninth grade year. As a group of high school seniors, they ranked very high in their respective school classes and appeared to be representative of top high school students throughout the state. A complete description of criteria used in their selection and of the Laboratory program can be found elsewhere (Rothney & Sanborn, 1966).

Treatments

On the day they made their annual visit to the Laboratory, subjects from each of the 17 schools were randomly assigned to three treatment groups. The number of subjects to receive each treatment on a given day varied from four to six, depending on the number of students each school sent to the Laboratory.

During a half-hour period immediately prior to the informational interview, two male Laboratory staff counselors administered one of three different treatments to each small group. The two counselors had master's degrees in counseling and guidance and each had several years of counseling experience in secondary schools. The researchers attempted to equalize the effect of the counselor variable among the treatments by assigning counselors to the treatment groups on a rotating basis. The three treatments were administered as follows:

Cue Presentation Plus Systematic Reinforcement (CPR). The counselor explained the purpose of meeting as a group in the following manner:

We have arranged for you to visit with a professor who teaches in the academic area in which you have indicated an interest. Our purpose now is to help each of you get some ideas for your interviews. The professors have indicated that the interviews are best when students come to their offices with some specific questions in mind. You will find paper and pencils on the table in front of you. If you wish, you may jot down any of the questions we cover and take them along to the interview. Before we begin, I would be interested in knowing the career or academic area you plan to investigate today.

After each student identified his area of interest, the counselor continued:

Perhaps the best way we can prepare for your professor visit is to discuss some questions that you could ask the professor during your interview with him. Does anyone have a question in mind?

Throughout the remainder of the group session, the counselor encouraged students to verbalize possible questions worth asking their professors. The counselor reinforced each question by verbally recognizing and/or indicating approval (e.g., "good," "an excellent question," "I think that's a legitimate question to ask"). The counselor also used cue questions designed to elicit student responses that could be reinforced:

1. What else do people generally want to know about an academic area or vocation?
2. What might you ask the professor about training for a job in this area?
3. What are some questions you would want to raise with the professor concerning the future outlook of this field?

The counselor closed the group session by encouraging students to make the best possible use of the interview by asking appropriate questions and by taking along any questions they wrote down during the group session. Twenty-three subjects (8 boys and 15 girls) were given the CPR treatment.

Social Model Plus Reinforcement (SMR). This treatment was introduced by the same manner as the CPR treatment. After determining each student's area of interest the counselor said:

Perhaps the best way we can prepare for your professor visit is to see a videotape of how one senior boy approached his professor, and to listen to some of his questions. The student in this videotape is Steve ...., a senior at James Madison Memorial High School. Steve is active in sports, a member of Memorial's newspaper staff, and an elected member of the National Honor Society. We will observe Steve as he visits with Dr. ...., a professor of electrical engineering at the University of Wisconsin. We feel Steve asks Dr. .... some good questions that enable him to learn a great deal about the field of electrical engineering. After viewing the interview, we can identify some of the questions that you think might be appropriate for your own interviews with University professors.

The student then reviewed a 14-minute videotape of the interview between Steve and a University of Wisconsin professor in electrical engineering, a live interview taped the previous year. No script had been prepared for the interview but the authors did provide Steve with a number of questions he could ask. The professor had been encouraged to express approval of Steve's questions.

Following the videotape presentation, a 10-minute period was provided for discussion and reinforcement. The counselor asked cue questions such as:

1. What were some of the questions that Steve asked Dr. .... which might be appropriate for you to ask your professor?
2. What else did Steve ask Dr. ....?
3. Can you think of any questions Steve neglected to ask but which might be appropriate for you to ask?

The counselor concluded the group session by encouraging the students to take along questions they might have recorded and to ask any questions they felt relevant during their professor visits. Twenty-three subjects (10 boys and 13 girls) were given this treatment.

Traditional Group Discussion (TGD). The counselor administered this treatment in exactly the same manner as the CPR treatment, except that he refrained from systematically reinforcing student responses. The counselor provided the same cues as were used in the CPR treatments to structure the group discussion. An attempt to stimulate discussion was made through the use of reflection, clarification, and summarization. Whenever possible, the counselor called upon students to clarify and to summarize the content of the group discussion. They were encouraged to take notes and refer to them during the professor visit. Twenty-five students (11 boys and 14 girls) were given this treatment.

Criteria Collection and Validation

The criterion behavior was defined as the frequency of student information-seeking behavior in the form of questions (ISQ) that students raised during interviews with University of Wisconsin professors immediately following the group sessions. Upon returning to the Laboratory from their professor visits, students were asked to respond to a questionnaire concerning their interviews. The questionnaire consisted of 28 items identified by the authors to be relevant questions concerning any academic area or career. The students were asked to indicate which of these 28 questions had been discussed during the interview. They were also given the opportunity to list any additional questions that had been discussed.

Although student self-reports have been found to be highly reliable both at the Laboratory and elsewhere (Davis, 1970; Krumboltz & Schroeder, 1965; Krumboltz & Thoresen, 1964), it was deemed desirable to validate a random sample of questionnaires. To accomplish this, the professors interviewed by 11 seniors (15 percent of all subjects) were asked to respond to the same questionnaire immediately afterward. Of the 146 questions these 11 students indicated had been discussed, 111 were verified by the professors. Thus, 76 percent of the questions these subjects reported as being discussed were actually validated by the professors.

Hypotheses

The following were tested:

1. There are no statistically significant differences in numbers of questions asked during visits by subjects in the three treatment groups.
2. There is no statistically significant difference between boys and girls in the number of questions asked during visits.
3. There is no statistically significant interaction between the main effects of treatment and sex.

The level of significance for this study was set at .25 to increase the probability of detecting main and interaction effects. Conventional levels of significance were considered too insensitive to differences that might exist between three "active" treatments. According to Winer (1962):

The frequent use of the .05 and .01 levels of significance is a matter of convention having little scientific logical basis. When the power of tests is likely to be low under these levels of significance, and when the type 1 and type 2 errors are approximately equal in importance, the .30 and .20 levels of significance may be more appropriate than the .05 and .01 levels [p. 13].

In view of the current Laboratory policy of providing some type of preparation for the professor visit, it was felt that accepting a false hypothesis would be no more or less serious an error than rejecting a true hypothesis. Also, the power for testing the hypotheses was limited since the sample size was relatively small and the population variance was likely to be large. The level of significance was therefore set to increase the probability of detecting significant main effects, and hypotheses were rejected at the .25 level of significance.

Results

Tape recordings were made of the five CPR and six TGD group sessions to determine whether the two treatments were actually different. Two independent judges who were unaware of the treatments involved evaluated the tape recordings by making frequency counts of counselor cue questions and counselor verbal reinforcements. Table 1 indicates the mean number of times counselors asked cue questions and offered verbal reinforcements for appropriate student responses during the CPR and TGD treatments. The data in Table 1 supported the idea that CPR and TGD treatments were actually different.

A 3x2 fixed effects analysis of variance was computed using treatment and sex as main effect factors. As Table 2 indicates, both main effects reached at least the .25 level of significance. The interaction effects were not significant and appear to be negligible.

The null hypothesis that treatment

Table 1

Mean Frequency of Counselor Cue Questions and Verbal
Reinforcements for CPR and TGD Treatments

Counselor Interaction	Treatment	
	CPR	TGD
Cue questions	19.5	18.5
Verbal reinforcements	27.0	3.3

Table 2

Mean Frequency of ISQ by Treatment and Sex,
and Summary of Analysis of Variance of ISQ Frequency

Treatment	Mean Frequency		
	Male	Female	Total
CPR	17.00	15.93	16.30
SMR	15.70	13.92	14.70
TGD	14.55	13.21	13.80
Total	15.62	14.40	14.90

Source	df	SS	MS	F
Treatment	2	77.592	38.796	2.474**
Sex of subject	1	32.827	32.827	2.094*
Interaction	2	1.456	.728	.046
Error (within)	67	1050.456	15.678	
Total	70	1160.900		

$* p < .25.$
$** p < .10.$

groups would not differ on the criterion was rejected. As can be seen in Table 2, the CPR method was associated with the highest ISQ frequency, the SMR with the next highest, and the TGD with the lowest frequency. The null hypothesis of no difference between the number of ISQ reported by subjects according to sex was also rejected. No matter which treatment they received, boys asked more questions than girls.

The third null hypothesis was retained. No interaction between main effects was found. Apparently, then, none of the three treatments would be most effective for one sex but *not* most effective for the other.

Discussion

The results indicate that reinforcement can be effective in increasing the number of questions superior students ask professors during information-seeking interviews. This finding is significant because it suggests that use of verbal reinforcement by counselors is an effective means of encouraging high-achieving students to seek information relevant to their educational and vocational planning. High-achieving students may have an internalized reward system that distinguishes them from other students and that continually motivates them to work toward long-range, secondary goals, but immediate verbal reinforcement by significant others still seems a useful tool in shaping their short-range, goal-oriented behavior.

Contrary to earlier studies employing a dependent variable similar to the one used in this study (Krumboltz & Schroeder, 1965; Krumboltz & Thoresen, 1964; Meyer, Strowig, & Hosford, 1970), some evidence was found to suggest that reinforcement alone may be a more efficient method of increasing ISQ than the presentation of a social model followed by a brief reinforcement session, at least when a limited time period for treatment is stipulated. One plausible explanation for the differences between these two techniques in this study may be the subjects' "attending" behavior. While the videotape was being played, the students in the VTR treatment were observed to be concentrating on the screen and only infrequently were they observed recording questions for their professor visits. Contrastingly, students in the CPR and TGD treatments were observed to be recording questions throughout the sessions.

Another possible explanation for the difference found between the CPR and VTR groups concerns the limitations inherent in recorded social models. The students may have viewed some of the questions asked by the model as being too esoteric for them to generalize to their own situation. It is even possible that the model had little or no effect and that the short reinforcement period is responsible for increased ISQ. Research is needed that isolates the importance of the social model in model-reinforcement treatments.

One reason for the discrepancy between the mean number of ISQ as reported by both boys and girls may be the social-cultural pressure on boys to select a career during their senior year in high school. Senior girls may not visualize the forthcoming college experience in terms of a career and may, therefore, be less inclined to ask questions related to occupations. The girls may have confined many of their questions to inquiries about the academics of college while boys asked academically *and* vocationally oriented questions. If this hypothesis is supported by future research, it will have implications for counselors preparing students for interviews with college officials.

References

Davis, J. L. Actions taken on counselors' suggestions as reported by four groups of academically superior high school students. Unpublished doctoral dissertation, University of Wisconsin, 1970.

Gelatt, H. B. Decision-making: A conceptual frame of reference for guidance and counseling. *Journal of Counseling Psychology*, 1962, *9*, 240–245.

Krumboltz, J. D., & Schröeder, W. W. Promoting career planning through reinforcement and models. *Personnel and Guidance Journal*, 1965, *44*, 19–26.

Krumboltz, J. D., & Thoresen, C. E. The effect of behavioral counseling in group and individual settings on information-seeking behavior. *Journal of Counseling Psychology*, 1964, *11*, 324–333.

Krumboltz, J. D., & Thoresen, C. E. *Behavioral counseling: Cases and techniques.* New York: Holt, Rinehart & Winston, 1969.

Krumboltz, J. D., Varenhorst, B. B., & Thoresen, C. E. Nonverbal factors in the effectiveness of models in counseling. *Journal of Counseling Psychology*, 1967, *14*, 412–418.

Meyer, J. B., Strowig, W., & Hosford, R. E. Behavioral-reinforcement counseling with rural high school youth. *Journal of Counseling Psychology*, 1970, *17*, 127–132.

Rothney, J. W. M. *Guidance practices and results.* New York: Harper, 1958.

Rothney, J. W. M., & Sanborn, M. P. Wisconsin's research - through - service program for superior high school students. *Personnel and Guidance Journal*, 1966, *44*, 694–699.

Winer, B. J. *Statistical principles in experimental design.* New York: McGraw-Hill, 1962.

THE APPLICATION OF OPERANT CONDITIONING TECHNIQUES IN A SECONDARY SCHOOL CLASSROOM

Loring W. McAllister, James G. Stachowiak,
Donald M. Baer, and Linda Conderman

Numerous studies have reported the effectiveness of operant conditioning techniques in modifying the behavior of children in various situations. Harris, Wolf, and Baer (1964), in a series of studies on pre-school children, described the effectiveness of contingent teacher attention in modifying inappropriate behavior. Hall and Broden (1967), Patterson (1965), Rabb and Hewett (1967), and Zimmerman and Zimmerman (1962) have demonstrated the usefulness of teacher-supplied contingent social reinforcement in reducing problem behaviors and increasing appropriate behaviors of young children in special classrooms. Becker, Madsen, Arnold, and Thomas (1967); Hall, Lund, and Jackson (1968); and Madsen, Becker, and Thomas (1968) extended these techniques into the regular primary school classroom and demonstrated their effectiveness there. In all of the above studies, only a limited number of children were studied in each situation, usually one or two per classroom.

Thomas, Becker, and Armstrong (1968) studied the effects of varying teachers' social behaviors on the classroom behaviors of an entire elementary school classroom of 28 students. By observing 10 children per session, one at a time, they demonstrated the effectiveness of approving teacher responses in maintaining appropriate classroom behaviors. Bushell, Wrobel, and Michaelis (1968) also applied group contingencies (special events contingent on earning tokens for study behaviors) to an entire class of 12 preschool children.

There has been an effort to extend the study of teacher-supplied consequences to larger groups of preschool and elementary school subjects in regular classrooms, but no systematic research investigating these procedures has yet been undertaken in the secondary school classroom. Cohen, Filipczak, and Bis (1967) reported the application of various non-social contingencies (earning points, being "correct", and taking advanced educational courses) in modifying attitudinal and academic behaviors of adolescent inmates in a penal institution. But there is no record of investigations into the effects of teacher-supplied social consequences on the classroom behavior of secondary school students in regular classrooms.

At present, the usefulness of contingent teacher social reinforcement in the management of student classroom behaviors is well documented on the preschool and primary elementary school levels, particularly when the

JOURNAL OF APPLIED BEHAVIOR ANALYSIS, 1969, Vol. 2, pp. 277-285.

investigation focuses on a limited number of children in the classroom. Systematic replication now requires that these procedures be extended to larger groups of students in the classroom and to students in the upper elementary and secondary grades. The present study sought to investigate the effects of teacher-supplied social consequences on the classroom behaviors of an entire class of secondary school students.

METHOD

Subjects

Students. The experimental group was a low-track, junior-senior English class containing 25 students (12 boys and 13 girls). At the beginning of the study the ages ranged from 16 to 19 yr (mean 17.11 yr); I.Q.s ranged from 77 to 114 (mean 94.43). Approximately 80% of the students were from lower-class families; the remainder were from middle-class families. The control group was also a low-track, junior-senior English class of 26 students (13 boys and 13 girls). The ages ranged from 16 to 19 yr (mean 17.04 yr); I.Q.s ranged from 73 to 111 (mean 91.04). About 76% of these students were from lower-class families, 16% were from middle-class families and 4% were from upper-middle to upper-class families. The experimental class met in the mornings for a 70-min period and the control class met in the afternoons for a 60-min period.

Teacher. The teacher was 23 yr old, female, middle class, and held a Bachelor's degree in education. She had had one year's experience in teaching secondary level students, which included a low-track English class. She taught both the experimental and control classes in the same classroom and utilized the same curriculum content for both. She stated that she had been having some difficulties in controlling classroom behavior in both classes and volunteered to cooperate in the experiment in the interest of improving her teaching-management skills. She stated that she had been able to achieve some rapport with these students during the two months that school had been in session. She described the students, generally, as performing poorly in academic work and ascribed whatever academic behaviors she was able to observe in them as being the result of her rapport with them. She stated that she was afraid that she would destroy this rapport if she attempted to exercise discipline over inappropriate classroom behaviors.

Procedures

The basic design utilized was the common pretest-posttest control group design combined with the use of a multiple baseline technique (Baer, Wolf, and Risley, 1968) in the experimental class.

Target behaviors. Both classes were observed for two weeks to ascertain general occurrence rates of various problem behaviors that had been described by the teacher. Inappropriate talking and turning around were selected as target behaviors because of their relatively high rate of occurrence. Inappropriate talking was defined as any audible vocal behavior engaged in by a student without the teacher's permission. Students were required to raise their hands to obtain permission to talk, either to the teacher or to other students, except when general classroom discussions were taking place, in which cases a student was not required to obtain permission to talk if his statements were addressed to the class and/or teacher and were made within the context of the discussion. Inappropriate turning was defined as any turning-around behavior engaged in by any student while seated in which he turned more than 90 degrees in either direction from the position of facing the front of the room. Two exceptions to this definition were made: turning behavior observed while in the process of transferring material to or from the book holder in the bottom of the desk was considered appropriate, as was any turning that took place when a student had directly implied permission to turn around. Examples of the latter exception would be when the class was asked to pass papers up or down the rows of desks, or when students turned to look at another student who was talking appropriately in the context of a recitation or discussion.

Observation and recording. Behavior record forms were made up for recording observed target behaviors in both classes. A portion of the form is illustrated in Fig. 1. The forms for the experimental class contained 70 sequentially numbered boxes for each behavior; the forms for the control class contained 60 sequentially numbered boxes for each behavior (covering the 70- and 60-min class periods, respectively). The occurrence of a target behavior during any minute interval of time (*e.g.,* during the twenty-fifth minute of class time) was recorded by placing a check mark in the appropriate box for that interval (*e.g.*, box 25) beside the behavior listed. Further occurrences of that behavior during that particular interval were not recorded. Thus, each time interval represented a dichotomy with respect to each behavior: the behavior had or had not occurred during that interval of time. A daily quantified measurement of each behavior was obtained by dividing the number of intervals that were checked by the total number of intervals in the class period, yielding a percentage of intervals in which the behavior occurred at least once. Time was kept by referral to a large, easily readable wall clock whose minute hand moved 1 min at a time.

Behaviors were recorded daily during all conditions by the teacher. Reliability of observation was checked by using from one to two additional observers (student teachers and the senior author) who visited the classes twice per week. Students in this particular school were thought to be quite accustomed to observers, due to the large amount of classroom observation done there by student teachers from a nearby university. Except for the senior author and teacher, other observers were not made aware of changes in experimental conditions. Reliability was assessed by comparing the behavior record forms of the teacher and observers after each class period in which both teacher and observers recorded behavior. A percentage of agreement for each target behavior was computed, based on a ratio of the number of intervals on which all recorders agreed (*i.e.*, that the behavior had or had not occurred) to the total number of intervals in the period. Average reliability for talking behavior was 90.49% in the experimental class (range 74 to 98%) and 89.49% in the control class (range 78 to 96%). Average reliability for turning behavior was 94.27% in the experimental class (range 87 to 98%) and 90.98% in the control class (range 85 to 96%).

In addition, two aspects of the teacher's be-havior were recorded during all conditions by the observers when present: (a) the number of inappropriate talking or turning instances that occasioned a verbal reprimand from the teacher, and (b) the number of direct statements of praise dispensed by the teacher for appropriate behaviors. These behaviors were recorded by simply tallying the number of instances in which they were observed on the reverse side of the observer's form. Reliability between observers was checked by computing a percentage of agreement between them on the number of instances of each type of behavior observed. Average reliability for reprimand behavior was 92.78% in the experimental class (range 84 to 100%) and 94.84% in the control class (range 82 to 100%). Average reliability for praise behavior was 98.85% in the experimental class (range 83 to 100%) and 97.65% in the control class (range 81 to 100%).

Baseline Condition. During the Baseline Condition, the two target behaviors and teacher behaviors were recorded in both the experimental and control classes. The teacher was asked to behave in her usual manner in both classrooms and no restrictions were placed on any disciplinary techniques she wished to use. The Baseline Condition in the experimental class was continued for 27 class days (approximately five weeks) to obtain as clear a picture as possible of the student and teacher behaviors occurring.

Experimental Condition I. This first experimental condition began in the experimental class on the twenty-eighth day when the teacher initiated various social consequences contingent on inappropriate talking behavior aimed at lowering the amount of this behavior taking place. The procedures agreed upon with the teacher for the application of social consequences were as follows:

(1) The teacher was to attempt to disapprove of all instances of inappropriate talking behavior whenever they occurred with a direct, verbal, sternly given reproof. Whenever possible, the teacher was to use students' names when

Minute No.	1	2	3	4	5	6	7	8	9	10	11	12	13	14	15	16	17	18	19	20	21
Talking																					
Turning																						

Fig. 1. Portion of behavior record form used to record incidence of target behavior.

correcting them. The teacher was instructed not to mention any other inappropriate behavior (*e.g.*, turning around) that might also be occurring at the time. Examples of reprimands given were: "John, be quiet!", "Jane, stop talking!", "Phil, shut up!", "You people, be quiet!". It was hypothesized that these consequences constituted an aversive social consequence for inappropriate talking.

(2) The teacher was asked not to threaten students with or apply other consequences, such as keeping them after school, exclusion from class, sending them to the Assistant Principal, *etc.* for inappropriate talking or for any other inappropriate behavior.

(3) The teacher was to praise the entire class in the form of remarks like: "Thank you for being quiet!", "Thank you for not talking!", or "I'm delighted to see you so quiet today!" according to the following contingencies: (a) During the first 2 min of class, praise at the end of approximately each 30-sec period in which there had been no inappropriate talking. (b) During the time in which a lecture, recitation, or class discussion was taking place, praise the class at the end of approximately each 15-min period in which no inappropriate talking had occurred. (c) When silent seatwork had been assigned, do not interrupt the period to praise, but praise the class at the end of the period if no inappropriate talking had occurred during the period. (d) At the end of each class make a summary statement concerning talking behavior, such as: "Thank you all for being so quiet today!", or "There has been entirely too much talking today. I'm disappointed in you!", or, "You have done pretty well in keeping quiet today, let's see if you can do better tomorrow!".

The concentration of praising instances during the first 2-min of class was scheduled because the baseline data revealed inappropriate talking as particularly frequent at this time.

Although the teacher continued to record instances of turning behavior, she was instructed to ignore this behavior in the experimental class during Experimental Condition I. In effect, baseline recording of turning behavior continued during this Condition. No changes were made in the teacher's behavior in the control class.

Experimental Condition II. After Experimental Condition I had been in effect in the experimental class for 26 class days and had

markedly reduced talking behavior (see Results), Experimental Condition II was put into effect on the fifty-fourth day of the study. In this condition, the contingent social consequences for talking behavior in the experimental class were continued and, in addition, the teacher initiated the same system of contingent social consequences for turning behavior, with the aim of reducing the amount of this behavior occurring. This subsequent provision of similar consequences, first for one behavior and then for another, constitutes the multiple baseline technique.

The procedures agreed upon for providing reprimands for inappropriate turning behavior were the same as those for talking behaviors, except that the teacher referred to "turning" instead of "talking" in her reproofs. She could now also mention both behaviors in her reproof if a student happened to be doing both. The procedures regarding the application of praise contingent on not turning around were also the same as before, except that the higher frequency of praising during the first 2 min of class was not used. Also, the teacher could now combine her positive remarks about not talking and not turning if such were appropriate to existing conditions. Finally, since inappropriate talking behavior had been reduced considerably by this time, the procedure of praising every 30 sec during the first 2-min of class was dropped. As before, no changes were made in the teacher's behavior in the control class.

RESULTS

Because data were not collected on individual students, it is not possible to specify exactly how many students were involved in either inappropriate talking or turning behavior. The observers and teacher agreed that over one-half of the students in both classes were involved in inappropriate talking behavior and that about one-third of the students in both classes were involved in inappropriate turning behavior.

Talking Behavior

Figure 2 indicates the daily percentages of intervals of inappropriate talking behavior in the experimental and control classes throughout the study. During the Baseline Condition in the experimental class and the equivalent period in the control class (Days 1 through 27), the average daily percentage of inappropriate talking intervals was 25.33% in the experimental class and 22.81% in the control class. The two classes were thus approximately equivalent with respect to the amount of inappropriate talking behavior in each before the experimental interventions were made in the experimental class. As can be seen, the introduction of the contingencies in Experimental Condition I on Day 28 immediately reduced the percentage of intervals of inappropriate talking behavior in the experimental class. From this point on, the amount of inappropriate talking behavior in the experimental class continued to decrease and finally stabilized at a level below 5%. Meanwhile, the control class continued to manifest its previous level of inappropriate talking behavior. In the period from Day 28 through Day 62, when the study was concluded, the average daily percentage of inappropriate talking intervals in the control class was 21.51%, compared with an average of 5.34% in the experimental class.

Turning Behavior

The results obtained with the second target behavior, inappropriate turning around, can be seen in Fig. 3, which indicates the daily percentages of intervals of inappropriate turning

behavior in both classes during the study. During the Baseline Condition in the experimental class and the equivalent period in the control class (Days 1 through 53), the level of inappropriate turning behavior was slowly increasing in both classes. The average daily percentage of inappropriate turning intervals during this time was 15.13% in the experimental class and 14.45% in the control class. As with talking behavior, the two classes were roughly equivalent in the amount of inappropriate turning behavior observed before experimental interventions were made. The introduction of Experimental Condition II contingencies on Day 54 again immediately reduced the percentage of inappropriate turning intervals in the experimental class. This behavior continued to decrease during the remaining days of the study. In the control class, the level of inappropriate turning behavior remained essentially the same. In the period from Day 54 through Day 62, the average daily percentage of inappropriate turning intervals in the control class was 17.22% and in the experimental class was 4.11%.

Teacher Behavior

During the Baseline period on talking behavior, the average number of instances of in-

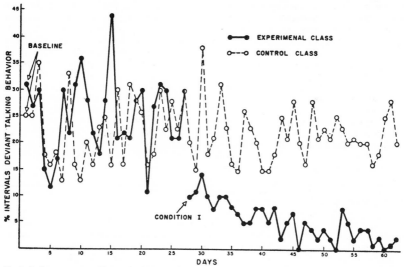

Fig. 2. Daily percentages of intervals of inappropriate talking behavior in experimental and control classes during Baseline and Experimental Condition I periods.

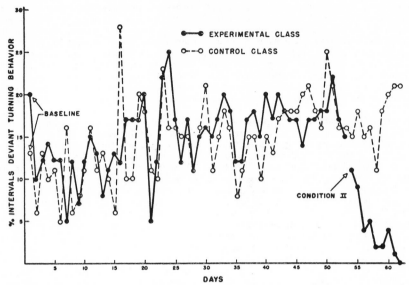

Fig. 3. Daily percentages of intervals of inappropriate turning behavior in experimental and control classes during Baseline and Experimental Condition II periods.

appropriate talking per class period that received some type of verbal reprimand from the teacher was 25.76% in the experimental class and 22.23% in the control class. The majority of these verbal responses took the form of saying, "Shhh!". On occasion, observers noted that the teacher corrected students directly, using their names. On several occasions she made general threats, stating that she would keep people after school if talking did not subside; however, she was never observed to carry out this kind of threat. During this period there were no observations of the teacher's dispensing any praise for not talking. During Experimental Condition I, the teacher disapproved of an average of 93.33% of inappropriate talking instances per class period in the experimental class. In the control class during this time, she disapproved of an average of 21.38% of inappropriate talking instances per class period. She also praised on an average of 6.07 occasions per experimental class period, contingent on not talking, during this time. With two exceptions, she was not observed directly to praise not talking in the control class.

During the Baseline period on inappropriate turning behavior, the average percentage

of inappropriate turning instances per class period that received verbal reprimands from the teacher was 12.84% in the experimental class and 13.09% in the control class. Most of these were simple instructions, like, "Turn around!", and she used the student's name in most cases. During Experimental Condition II, the average percentage of inappropriate turning instances per class period that occasioned disapproving responses from the teacher was 95.50% in the experimental class and 18.50% in the control class. In addition, she praised on an average of 5.75 occasions per experimental class period, contingent on not turning. In the control class she was not observed to provide any such praise for not turning.

DISCUSSION

The results indicate quite clearly that the statements of praise and disapproval by the teacher had consistent effects on the two target behaviors observed in the experimental class. Both behaviors decreased. That the statements were, in fact, responsible for the observed modifications in behavior was demonstrated through the multiple baseline procedure in which the target behaviors changed maximally only when the statements were applied. The use of the control class data further substantiates this contention. The observations of teacher behavior in the study provide evidence that the program was being carried out as specified in the two classrooms.

The design of the study does not make it possible to isolate the separate effects of the teacher's statements of praise and disapproval on the students' behaviors. It is possible that one or the other of these was more potent in achieving the observed results. In addition to the possibility that statements of praise or disapproval, in themselves, might have differed in their effectiveness in modifying behavior, the different manner in which these two types of statements were delivered may have resulted in differing effects. The design, it will be remembered, called for disapproving statements to be delivered to individual students, while praise was delivered to the class as a whole. This resulted in a sudden onset of numerous disapproving statements delivered to individual students when Experimental Condition I was put into effect. The observers agreed that the students seemed "stunned" when this essentially radical shift in stimulus conditions took place. The immediate and marked decrease in inappropriate talking behavior at this point may have resulted because of this shift. The phenomenon can be compared to the sudden response rate reductions observed in animals when stimulus conditions are shifted suddenly. The decrease in inappropriate turning behavior observed when Experimental Condition II was put into effect, while immediate, was not of the same magnitude as that observed previously. Perhaps some measure of adaptation to this type of stimulus shift had taken place. Regardless of the possible reasons for the immediate effects observed when the experimental conditions were put into effect, it is also true that the direction of these effects was maintained thereafter in both experimental conditions. The combination of praise and disapproval undoubtedly was responsible for this.

Assuming that praise statements were functioning as positive reinforcers for a majority of the experimental class, they may have operated not only directly to reinforce behaviors incompatible with inappropriate talking and turning but also to generate peer-group pressure to reduce inappropriate behavior because such statements were contingent on the entire class' behavior. Further studies are needed to investigate the effects of peer-group contingencies on individual behavior.

Although it appears that the statements of praise and disapproval by the teacher functioned as positive reinforcers and punishers, respectively, an alternative possibility exists. These statements may have been operating primarily as instructions that the students complied with. It is conceivable that had praise statements, for example, been delivered as instructions independent of the occurrence of inappropriate behavior the same results might have been obtained. Also, it should be noted that results obtained in other studies (Lovaas, Freitag, Kinder, Rubenstein, Schaeffer, and Simmons, 1964; Thomas, Becker, and Armstrong, 1968) indicate that disapproving adult behaviors do not have a unitary effect on children's behavior. What would appear to be punishing types of statements are sometimes found to function as positive reinforcers. Informal observations indicated that this seemed to be the case in this study, at least as far as one student was concerned.

Several comments may be made regarding the practical aspects of the present approach. The study further exemplifies the usefulness of the multiple baseline technique, which makes it unnecessary to reverse variables in order to demonstrate the specific effectiveness of the experimental variables. Many teachers and school administrators will undoubtedly find this approach more acceptable in their schools. The notion of reversing variables to reinstitute what is considered to be maladaptive or inappropriate behavior is extremely repugnant to many educators who are more interested in "getting results" than in experimental verification of the results obtained.

The study differs from most previous operant research in classrooms in that the focus was on recording and modifying target behaviors without specific regard to the individual students involved. Most earlier studies have focused on observing the behavior of one student at a time. With this approach, it takes considerable time to extend observations to an entire class and usually this is not done. While observations of an entire class are not always necessary from a practical point of view (*i.e.*, only a few students are involved in inappropriate behaviors), the present approach does seem feasible when the number of students involved in one or more classes of inappropriate behavior is large. From an experimental point of view, this study was deficient in not providing more exact information as to the number of students actually involved in the target behaviors. Once this facet is determined, however, the essential approach seems quite feasible and practical.

It might be argued that a group-oriented approach will not function in the same way with all members of the group. This is potentially possible, if not probable. However, two practical aspects should be considered. In the first place, such an approach could conceivably remediate the total situation enough to allow the teacher to concentrate on those students who either have not responded or who have become worse. Secondly, perhaps a general reduction in inappropriate behavior is all the teacher desires. In this study, for example, the results obtained were, according to the teacher, more than enough to satisfy her. She did not, in other words, set a criterion of eliminating the target behaviors.

A significant practical aspect of this study was the amount of difficulty encountered by the teacher in recording behavior and delivering contingent praise and disapproval. It might be asked how she found time to teach when she was involved in these activities. Perhaps the best judge of the amount of difficulty involved with these techniques is the teacher herself. She reported that, initially, recording behaviors was difficult. The task did take considerable time and did interrupt her on-going teaching. On the other hand, the large amount of talking and other inappropriate behaviors occurring at the beginning of the study also interrupted her teaching. She felt that as the study went on she became more accustomed to recording and it became easier for her to accomplish. She pointed out that the fact that she usually positioned herself at her desk or rostrum also made recording somewhat easier because the forms were readily available. This was her usual position in the classroom; she did not change to make recording easier. Considerable time was required to deliver contingent praise and disapproval at the beginning of the experimental conditions. This also tended to interrupt teaching tasks as far as the teacher was concerned. However, she felt that

this state of affairs did not last long because the target behaviors declined so immediately and rapidly. The overall judgment of the teacher was that the procedures of recording and dispensing contingent consequences did, indeed, interfere with her teaching but that the results obtained more than compensated for this. When the levels of inappropriate behavior had been lowered she felt she could carry out her teaching responsibilities much more efficiently and effectively than before. She felt strongly enough about the practicality and effectiveness of the techniques to present information and data on the study to her fellow teachers and to offer her services as a consultant to those who wanted to try similar approaches in their classrooms.

The senior author held frequent conferences with the teacher after class periods. The aim was to provide her with feedback regarding her performance in class. She was actively praised for appropriate modifications in her classroom behavior and for record-keeping behavior. Likewise, she was criticized for mistakes in her application of program contingencies.

Finally, the data of this experiment are considered significant by reason of the strong implication that teacher praise and disapproval can function to modify the behavior of high-school level students. This potentially extends the implications of earlier research accomplished on the pre-school and elementary levels.

REFERENCES

Baer, D. M., Wolf, M. M., and Risley, T. R. Some current dimensions of applied behavior analysis. *Journal of Applied Behavior Analysis*, 1968, 1, 91-97.

Becker, W. C., Madsen, C. H., Jr., Arnold, C. R., and Thomas, D. R. The contingent use of teacher attention and praise in reducing classroom behavior problems. *Journal of Special Education*, 1967, 1, 287-307.

Bushell, D., Jr., Wrobel, P. A., and Michaelis, M. L. Applying "group" contingencies to the classroom study behavior of preschool children. *Journal of Applied Behavior Analysis*, 1968, 1, 55-61.

Cohen, H. L., Filipczak, J., and Bis, J. S. *Case I: an initial study of contingencies applicable to special education.* Silver Spring, Md.: Educational Facility Press—Institute for Behavioral Research, 1967.

Hall, R. V. and Broden, M. Behavior changes in brain-injured children through social reinforcement. *Journal of Experimental Child Psychology*, 1967, 5, 463-479.

Hall, R. V., Lund, D., and Jackson, D. Effects of teacher attention on study behavior. *Journal of Applied Behavior Analysis*, 1968, 1, 1-12.

Harris, F. R., Wolf, M. M., and Baer, D. M. Effects of adult social reinforcement on child behavior. *Young Children*, 1964, **20**, 8-17.

Lövaas, O. I., Freitag, G., Kinder, M. I., Rubenstein, D. B., Schaeffer, B., and Simmons, J. B. *Experimental studies in childhood schizophrenia—establishment of social reinforcers.* Paper read at Western Psychological Assn., Portland, April, 1964.

Madsen, C. H., Becker, W. C., and Thomas, D. R. Rules, praise and ignoring: elements of elementary classroom control. *Journal of Applied Behavior Analysis*, 1968, **1**, 139-150.

Patterson, G. R. An application of conditioning techniques to the control of a hyperactive child. In L. P. Ullman and L. Krasner (Eds.), *Case studies in behavior modification.* New York: Holt, Rinehart & Winston, 1966. Pp. 370-375.

Rabb, E. and Hewett, F. M. Developing appropriate classroom behaviors in a severely disturbed group of institutionalized kindergarten-primary children utilizing a behavior modification model. *American Journal of Orthopsychiatry*, 1967, **37**, 313-314.

Thomas, D. R., Becker, W. C., and Armstrong, M. Production and elimination of disruptive classroom behavior by systematically varying teacher's behavior. *Journal of Applied Behavior Analysis*, 1968, **1**, 35-45.

Zimmerman, E. H. and Zimmerman, J. The alteration of behavior in a special classroom situation. *Journal of the Experimental Analysis of Behavior*, 1962, **5**, 59-60.

SECTION FOUR

APPLICATIONS TO ACADEMIC PERFORMANCE

Perhaps the primary objective to any educational strategy ought to be improvement of academic performance. It would not be sufficient simply to demonstrate that a technique causes students to sit straighter, throw fewer paper wads, and get in less trouble at school. If the technique does not ultimately result in students' reading better, becoming more adept in solving math problems, or producing more creative themes, its long-range utility would be questionable.

The cruel facts are that most operant techniques have not been applied to academic indices. These procedures have unequivocally demonstrated their effectiveness in altering classroom social conduct. But can we assume that social conduct will be accompanied by improvement in academic achievement? Kirby and Shields' and Webb and Cormier's studies suggest some tentative answers to this question. The major question, of course, is how successful have operant techniques been when applied directly to academic performance. Articles by Clark and Walberg (1968) and Webb and Cormier (1972) provide definitive evidence that behavior management procedures can be highly effective in modifying academic performance. These articles deal with arrangements such as behavioral objectives, criterion referenced measurement, contingency contracts, and teacher approval. The study by Nolen, Kunzelmann, and Haring (1967) illustrates how behavioral strategies used to increase academic achievement in a special classroom generalized to regular classroom settings.

MODIFICATION OF ARITHMETIC RESPONSE RATE
AND ATTENDING BEHAVIOR IN A
SEVENTH-GRADE STUDENT[1]

Frank D. Kirby and Frank Shields

Recent studies have shown that operant conditioning techniques can be useful in improving children's classroom behaviors. Several of these studies have focused on either increasing study behavior or increasing academic response rate. Hall, Lund, and Jackson (1968) demonstrated that study behavior is subject to teacher attention contingencies. Bushell, Wrobel, and Michaelis (1968) modified study behavior utilizing a token system and group contingencies. Walker and Buckley (1968) conditioned attending behavior by providing points for increasing intervals of attending behavior. The points could be exchanged for a model of choice at the end of the treatment period. Surratt, Ulrich, and Hawkins (1969) utilized an elementary student to monitor the study behavior of a group of students. A light on the student's desk was on during study behavior and off during non-study behavior. Using back up rein-

forcers for light-on time, they increased time spent in study.

The main purpose of increasing study behavior is to achieve collateral increases in academic performance. The forementioned studies modified attending or study behavior but did not systematically measure changes in academic response rate or accuracy. One of the problems in attempting to increase academic response rate indirectly by modifying study behavior is the time and effort involved in monitoring study behavior. Someone must monitor the behavior of the child almost constantly. A more direct approach to academic performance may be more efficient.

Academic response rate has been directly modified by Lovitt and Curtiss (1968, 1969). These studies demonstrated increases in academic response rate as a result of verbalizing in addition to writing correct answers and of self-imposed as opposed to teacher-imposed reinforcement contingencies. Changes in percentage of study behavior were not systematically measured.

The present study was designed to measure the combined effects of an adjusting fixed-ratio schedule of immediate praise and immediate correctness feedback on the arithmetic response rate of a seventh-grade student and to measure

[1]This study is based on a thesis submitted to the Department of Psychology, Humboldt State College, in partial fulfillment of the requirements of the Master of Arts degree. The authors wish to express appreciation to Dr. Paul Ness of the College Elementary School, without whose cooperation this study would not have been possible.

JOURNAL OF APPLIED BEHAVIOR ANALYSIS, 1972, Vol. 5, pp. 79-84.

114

possible collateral changes in study behavior. The subject was rewarded for increasing units of arithmetic work in a manner similar to the procedure used by Walker and Buckley (1968) wherein the subject was rewarded for increasing intervals of time spent in study.

METHOD

Subject

Tom, a 13-yr-old boy enrolled in the seventh grade at Humboldt State College Elementary School, was of average intelligence as measured by the Wechsler Intelligence Scale for Children, receiving a Full Scale Score of 96. Before the study, Tom was observed for a period of two weeks. During this time, he exhibited a great deal of non-attending behavior and his arithmetic work was poor. Tom frequently exhibited non-attending behavior until his teacher reminded him to work or went over to his desk and watched him. Tom would then work for a few minutes, but if his teacher left, he would become easily distracted. Tom seldom completed class assignments and tended to make many errors, especially with arithmetic problems.

Procedure

After consultation with Tom's teacher, it was decided to use a 20-min time block each day in an experiment designed to help Tom increase his arithmetic achievement and attending be-

havior. The study was conducted in Tom's normal classroom every day from 11:30 to 11:50 a.m. During this time the experimenter presented Tom with a worksheet consisting of 20 multiplication problems to compute. Examples of the types of problems used are shown in Table 1. Complexity order #1 represents a one digit number times another one digit number (1×1) etc.

Random selection was used to determine the content for each worksheet. The problems were placed on individual cards and placed in one of nine boxes, each box contained problems of the same complexity. Two problems were drawn from each box for each of the 24 worksheets used during the study, giving each worksheet 18 problems. The remaining problems were then placed in one box and two more problems were selected for each of the 24 worksheets, so that each worksheet contained 20 problems. The problems were arranged in order of increasing complexity for each worksheet, i.e., 1×1, 1×2, 1×3, 2×1, 2×2, etc.

Two measures of behavior were recorded: the number of correct problems solved per minute and the percentage of total time spent in attending behavior. The number of correct problems solved was recorded by the experimenter each time Tom turned in a unit of work. The amount of time spent in problem solving included only the time he spent at his desk while completing the 20 problems and did not include

Table 1
Examples of the Multiplication Problems Used in the Present Study

Complexity Order	No. of Digits	Examples	Number
1.	1×1	2×6, 4×8	56
2.	1×2	3×12, 5×43	56
3.	1×3	8×754, 9×362	56
4.	2×1	54×7, 32×5	56
5.	2×2	34×65, 75×12	56
6.	2×3	23×143, 59×641	56
7.	3×1	645×4, 781×3	56
8.	3×2	893×34, 619×15	56
9.	3×3	156×723, 916×416 ...	56

the time he took to bring his work to the experimenter for correction, be assigned a new set of problems to solve, and return to his desk. Tom completed the entire worksheets of 20 problems each day of the experiment.

An independent observer was used to record Tom's attending behavior. The observer was seated in the classroom, approximately 18 ft from Tom's right-hand side, out of the way, but with an unobstructed view of the subject. From this position the observer recorded Tom's behavior every 10 sec, recording only behavior exhibited at the tenth second. The observer used a stopwatch, held in her left-hand, clearly marked, to determine the intervals. Attending behavior included: looking at or writing on the assigned page, looking at the teacher or experimenter when appropriate, talking to the teacher or experimenter, walking from his desk to the experimenter's desk and back to his own, and standing at the experimenter's desk while his paper was being corrected and a new assignment given. All other behavior was recorded as non-attending. If Tom completed the worksheet before the end of the assigned 20 min, the observer noted the time and stopped recording. This procedure was used throughout the study. The reliability of the observer was checked 10 times with another observer, three times before the start of the study and seven times during the study. The two observers sat in opposite corners at the rear of the room during reliability checks. The results showed a 98% agreement between observers, with a range from 95% to 100%. Percentage of agreement was determined by dividing the number of agreements by the total number of observations.

Design

The study was conducted over a period of 24 school days and was divided into four phases.

PHASE	DAYS
Baseline	1-5
Treatment 1	6-13
Reversal	14-19
Treatment 2	20-24

Baseline. During the baseline phase, Tom was presented each day with a different arithmetic worksheet of 20 problems His instructions were as follows:

> "Here is your arithmetic worksheet for today, you have 20 minutes to complete it, then I will collect it."

The problems were corrected and returned the following day with the number correct at the top. No praise was given Tom, by either the teacher or the experimenter during the 20-min period.

Treatment 1. During this phase, Tom was presented each day with a different arithmetic worksheet of 20 problems. The instructions given Tom during this phase were as follows:

> "Here is your arithmetic worksheet for today, when you have completed ____ problems, bring your paper over to my desk and I will check your answers. You have 20 minutes to complete the worksheet."

Tom was given praise and the correct answers marked subsequent to the correction of each unit of work using an adjusting fixed-ratio schedule. Initially this involved reinforcement for every two problems completed. Then, the experimenter gradually increased the units of work or number of problems completed by Tom before delivering reinforcement. Correct answers were designated but Tom was not shown how to work any problems or where he had made errors.

Examples of praise used by the experimenter included:

1. "Good work"
2. "Excellent job"
3. "Great, you got 14 right today"
4. "All right, you didn't do too well today, but tomorrow you will do better"
5. "Since you did so well today it won't be necessary to have your work checked as often tomorrow"

6. "And keep up the good work; you can work more problems at a time now"

For the first two days of Treatment 1, Days 6 and 7, Tom was given praise and the correct answers each time he completed two problems. During Days 8 and 9, the number of problems completed at one time was increased to four. Then, for Days 10 and 11, the number was increased to eight. Finally, for Days 12 and 13, no reinforcement was given until Tom had completed 16 problems.

Reversal. During this phase, Tom was given a different arithmetic worksheet of 20 problems each day with the same instructions used during baseline. His paper was corrected and returned the following day with the number correct at the top. No praise was given Tom by either the experimenter or the teacher.

Treatment 2. Each day, Tom was given a different arithmetic worksheet of 20 problems with the same instructions used during Treatment 1. Praise and correct answers were given Tom in the same manner as in Treatment 1, using an adjusting fixed-ratio schedule. The number of problems completed by Tom before presenting himself to the experimenter to have his work checked was increased from five for Day 20, to 10 for Day 21, 15 for Day 22, and all 20 problems for the last two days.

RESULTS

As can be seen in Figure 1, during baseline Tom's mean correct answer rate was 0.47 per

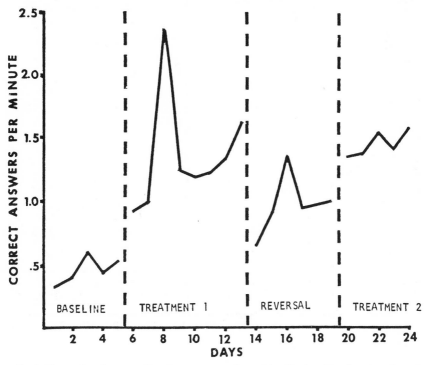

Fig. 1. The number of correct arithmetic answers per minute achieved by the subject throughout the study.

minute. During Treatment 1, the rate increased to a mean of 1.36 correct answers per minute. During reversal, the rate decreased to 0.98 and during Treatment 2, climbed to a mean of 1.44.

Collateral changes also occurred in attending behavior. Figure 2 shows that during baseline Tom spent a mean of 51% of his time in attending behavior. During Treatment 1, mean percentage of attending behavior rose sharply to 97%. There was a slight decrease during reversal to 82%, followed during Treatment 2 by an increase to 97%. It should be noted that Tom's behavior could not be recorded for Day 18 (reversal) because he left the room and completed the problems in the hallway.

DISCUSSION

The results demonstrate the combined effectiveness of the present adjusting fixed-ratio schedule of praise and immediate correctness feedback in increasing the subject's arithmetic response rate and associated attending behavior. When Tom's rate of correct problem solving was increased through systematic reinforcement, incompatible behaviors of non-attending decreased. It remains to be shown whether or not working directly on increasing attending behavior would have produced comparable improvement in arithmetic response rate.

One advantage of working directly on academic response rate instead of indirectly through

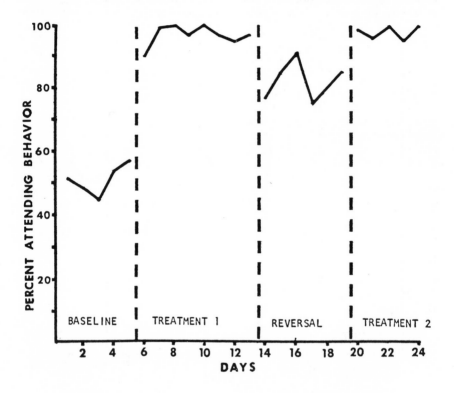

Fig. 2. Percentage of total time the subject spent in attending behavior throughout the study.

increasing attending behavior is the time and effort involved in monitoring the two forms of behavior. Working directly on arithmetic response rate, as in the present study, does not require the teacher constantly to monitor the student's study behavior. The only requirement of the teacher is immediately to correct the paper when presented and supply a short expression of praise upon returning the paper. While the adjusting ratio schedule of reinforcement requires frequent contact with the student during early phases requiring small units of work, it requires no extra effort during later phases when large units of work are assigned. The present study indicates that large units of work can be required rather quickly without deterioration in either academic response rate or related attending behavior. It is interesting to note that during reversal, when all praise and immediate correctness feedback was withheld, the subject maintained a much higher level of arithmetic achievement and attending behavior than before Treatment 1.

Though the praise and immediate correctness feedback were provided by the experimenter in this study, the classroom teacher, a selected pupil from the class (or even from another class), or a parent volunteer could easily perform the same function.

REFERENCES

Bushell, Don, Jr., Worbel, Patricia Ann, and Michaelis, Mary Louise. Applying "group" contingencies to the classroom study behavior of preschool children. *Journal of Applied Behavior Analysis*, 1968, 1, 55-61.

Hall, R. Vance; Lund, Diane, and Jackson, Deloris. Effects of teacher attention on study behavior. *Journal of Applied Behavior Analysis*, 1968, 1, 1-12.

Lovitt, Thomas C. and Curtiss, Karen A. Effects of manipulating an antecedent event on mathematics response rate. *Journal of Applied Behavior Analysis*, 1968, 1, 329-333.

Lovitt, Thomas C. and Curtiss, Karen A. Academic response rate as a function of teacher-and self-imposed contingencies. *Journal of Applied Behavior Analysis*, 1968, 1, 49-53.

Surratt, Paul R., Ulrich, Roger E., and Hawkins, Robert P. An elementary student as a behavior engineer. *Journal of Applied Behavior Analysis*, 1969, 2, 85-92.

Walker, Hill M. and Buckley, Nancy K. The use of positive reinforcement in conditioning attending behavior. *Journal of Applied Behavior Analysis*, 1968, 1, 245-252.

119

IMPROVING CLASSROOM BEHAVIOR AND ACHIEVEMENT

A. Bert Webb, Memphis State University

William H. Cormier, University of Tennessee

A great deal has been written about the merits of behavioral
objectives for classroom instruction. Ever since the publication of
Mager's Preparing Instructional Objectives (7), many curriculum leaders,
curriculum developers, programmers, and classroom teachers have prepared
and used behavioral objectives. Also, several researchers have investigated the effects of behavioral objectives on learning (1, 3, 4, 6, 10).
In all of these studies, the investigators assessed the effects of merely
establishing the behavioral objectives in writing as a function of the
instructional procedures. Criterion achievement tests were used to
assess the effectiveness of the objectives. None of the above studies
provided the opportunity for the subjects to engage in alternative
learning activities after deficiencies had been detected. This utiliza-
tion of alternatives is often referred to as prescriptive instruction
or remediation.

The primary purpose of this investigation was to study the
effects of behavioral objectives, criterion evaluation, and remediation
upon the classroom progress of disruptive adolescents. Classroom
behavior and academic achievement were examined within the experimental
setting.

JOURNAL OF EXPERIMENTAL EDUCATION, in press.

METHOD

Subjects

The subjects of this investigation were selected from four eighth grade general mathematics classes in a junior high school. Most of the subjects came from rural homes which were on a lower to middle socio-economic level. Two mathematics teachers, one male and one female, participated in the study. Each teacher selected two classes and identified the six most disruptive students in each class. The subjects for all four classes included 16 male and six female disruptive students.* Scores on the Otis-Lennon Mental Ability Test indicated that for this group of disruptive students the IQ scores ranged from 73 to 113 with a mean of 94. Group scores for mathematics achievement, based on the Metropolitan Achievement Test, revealed the following: range, third grade-second month (3.2) to ninth grade-ninth month (9.9); median achievement, sixth grade-sixth month (6.6).

PROCEDURE

Categories of Behavior

The following categories of classroom behavior were used:

Task Relevant (TR). Task relevant behavior included answering or asking questions which were lesson-oriented, writing or reading when directed to do so, hand raising to get the teacher's attention, looking at the teacher while he is lecturing, looking at another student who is

---

*Two of the original twenty-four students moved away during the progress of the investigation.

participating in lesson activity, and any other behavior which is consistent with the ongoing classroom activity.

Time Off Task (TO). This category included just sitting at one's desk without appropriate materials or without attempting to get appropriate materials. It was looking at non-lesson material, gazing out the window, or looking around the room when lesson activity had been assigned. The subject, however, was not distracting anyone else by his inattention.

Disruptive Behavior (DB). A rating of DB indicated that the subject had exhibited some behavior which disrupted the academic performance of another student. For example, motor behaviors were such behaviors as getting out of one's seat, standing up, walking around, rocking in one's chair, moving the chair, gesturing without talking, showing an object without talking, tapping another student to get his attention, throwing objects, or any other disruptive movement without noise. Also, tapping feet, clapping hands, tearing papers, tapping one's pencil on the desk, or any other nonverbal noise-producing behavior which was not directly involved in TR was rated as DB. Aggressive behaviors such as hitting, pushing, shoving, pinching, slapping, poking with objects, grabbing objects from another student, and destroying objects were rated as DB.

Observation and Recording

Observers used a 10-second time-sampling procedure to record the above categories of classroom behavior. The observer kept his eyes on the second hand of a stopwatch until the end of a 10-second time interval; then he looked up at the subject and recorded the behavior he observed. The observer then returned his eyes to the watch and kept them there until the end of the next 10-second interval. The observers were cautioned to record only one category of behavior during a 10-second interval. Each subject was observed for a total of six-minutes per class period. However, the observer recorded the behaviors of one subject for one-minute and then observed another subject for one-minute until all six subjects were observed. The observer repeated the cycle of observing each subject for one-minute six times. The sequence for observing the subjects was random for each cycle.

Observer Training and Reliability

The observers were instructed that they must be aware of class-room procedures in order to know that behavior was appropriate for a given situation. For example, the teacher may have allowed talking after students had finished their assignments. If the observers were not aware of such a situation, they may have recorded the subject's behavior incorrectly. Observers were also instructed not to interact with either pupils or teacher while in the classroom. They were repeatedly reminded to remain as unobtrusive as possible while in the classes. The observers were not informed about the purpose of the study or when changes in the experimental conditions occurred.

Reliability testing sessions simulated the actual classroom observation process which was described above. Videotapes of actual class sessions were used. As the observers watched the videotape, they recorded the classroom behaviors of designated pupils for a minimum of

123

18 minutes, or 108 10-second intervals. At the end of the reliability testing session, all data sheets were checked for agreement of ratings. If all observer ratings were not the same at a given interval, then agreement was not evident and the interval was counted incorrect. All incorrect ratings were then tabulated. If the combined incorrect ratings of the observers did not exceed 15 percent of the total number of behaviors recorded, then reliability was considered acceptable. If, however, the total number of incorrect responses was more than 15 percent of the total score, further training and review were given. Following the review session, another reliability test utilizing a new videotape was given. One test for observer reliability was conducted during each of the four experimental conditions of the investigation. After the training sessions, observer reliability was established at .88; the four subsequent sessions yielded reliability scores of .93, .95, .96, and .95.

Grader

In an attempt to insure impartiality in evaluating the subjects, all academic classroom work was scored by a trained grader. The participating teachers did not grade any academic material or tests. The grader was an experienced teacher who had a background in mathematics, and who was not employed at the site of the investigation. Essentially, the grader evaluated the work of the subjects according to the criteria established by the previously distributed behavioral objectives, and scored tests which were administered during the investigation. For example, pre- and posttests administered during Condition Two were scored by the grader. Also, the grader scored all tests given during the four conditions of the study. In this manner, an attempt was made to eliminate teacher bias in assignment of scores. The grader was not told the purpose of the study or when changes in the experimental conditions occurred.

Teacher Training

After the second week of Condition One, both teachers were given instruction in writing behavioral objectives and in developing criterion-referenced tests. They were then requested to prepare behavioral objectives for one unit which would account for approximately three weeks of the study and one covering about two weeks of work. The behavioral objectives were written so that a new set could be distributed to the students each day. The investigator examined each set of behavioral objectives for clarity and for inclusion of the essential conditions, activities, and expected levels of proficiency (5). The teachers were instructed also to construct a pretest and a posttest for use during Condition Two. Again, these instruments were examined by the investigator before they were administered. The teachers were instructed to provide all students an opportunity to remediate individually before initiating the use of a new set of objectives. Neither teacher was told the purpose of the study, and neither of them was given any information regarding the nature of the data that were recorded by the observers and the grader.

Experimental Design

The study consisted of four conditions (the first baseline, the first treatment, the second baseline, and the second treatment).

Condition One. Observers recorded behavioral data, and the grader scored academic classwork, homework, and mathematics tests. This condition lasted 12 school days. At the end of this condition both teachers were trained to write behavioral objectives, to teach lessons derived from the objectives, to use criterion-referenced measurement, and to provide alternative learning experiences.

Condition Two. The first treatment condition also lasted 12 school days. It was begun with the administration of a mathematics pretest covering a new unit of work for the subjects. Behavioral objectives were distributed daily by the teachers to all pupils in the selected classes. Free time was awarded to those pupils who successfully completed the assigned objectives for the given day. These pupils were also given the option to begin working on the next set of behavioral objectives. Those who were not successful in their attempt to meet the objectives were given the opportunity to engage in similar learning activities until they reached the prespecified goals. Then they moved to the next set of behavioral objectives. The mathematics posttest was administered at the end of this condition.

Condition Three. The second baseline condition lasted seven school days. The participating teachers were instructed to return to their pre-experimental way of instruction. They were reminded to refrain from using behavioral objectives, criterion evaluation, or remediation procedures.

Condition Four. The second treatment condition lasted five school days. Procedures in this condition were designed to replicate

those in condition two. An observer reliability testing session was
conducted in this condition, and in each of the previous three conditions.

RESULTS

Twenty-two eighth grade disruptive students from four classes
provided data for classroom behaviors (TR, TO, and DB) and academic
achievement (criterion tests) as a function of the four conditions of
the study. These data are presented in Figure I. The average percent
of TR, TO, and DB behaviors is depicted for each condition. Also,
Figure I shows the mean percent of achievement as measured by criterion
tests for the two baseline and the two treatment conditions.

The Friedman (nonparametric) two-way analysis of variance test
(9) revealed a significant chi-square for three degrees of freedom
(15.02, $p < .01$) for TR behaviors. Post hoc analysis of these data,
using the chi-square analog of Scheffe's Theorem (8), indicated significant differences ($p < .01$) between Conditions One and Two and between
Conditions One and Four. Examination of Figure I reveals that the mean
percentage of TR behaviors was greater under Condition Two than during
Condition One. The general level of TR behaviors established in
Condition Two was maintained during Condition Three. During Condition
Four, the frequency of TR behaviors increased, establishing a pattern
similar to that of Condition Two.

Using the Friedman two-way analysis of variance, TO behaviors were
found to be significantly different (chi-square 21.64, df = 3, $p < .01$).
Post hoc analysis indicated significant differences for TO behaviors
between Conditions One and Two ($p < .01$), between Conditions One and

FIGURE I

MEAN PERCENT OF CLASSROOM BEHAVIORS AND
ACHIEVEMENT OVER THE FOUR CONDITIONS
OF THE INVESTIGATION

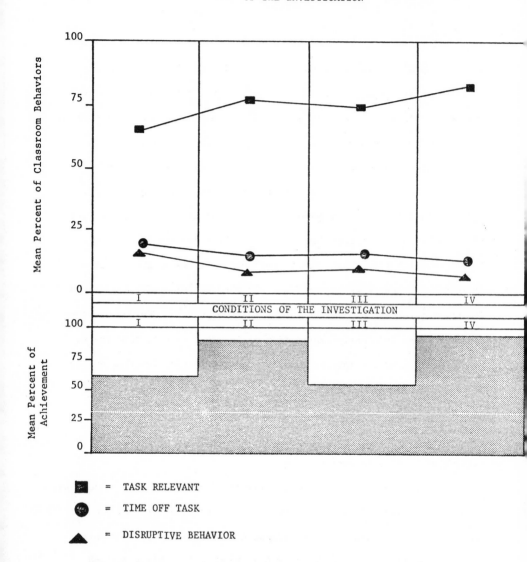

= TASK RELEVANT

= TIME OFF TASK

= DISRUPTIVE BEHAVIOR

Three (p $<$.05), and between Conditions One and Four (p $<$.01). As with TR behaviors, the general level of TO behaviors established in Condition Two was maintained for Condition Three. And during Condition Four, the frequency of TO behaviors decreased, establishing a pattern similar to that of Condition Two. There were no significant differences between the last three conditions of the study for TO behaviors.

The Friedman test for DB indicated that for a chi-square of 17.76, with df = 3, a significant difference was found (p $<$.01). Post hoc contrast of these data revealed differences in DB between Conditions One and Two (p $<$.05) and between Conditions One and Four (p $<$.01). Again, inspection of Figure 1 indicates that the same pattern existed for DB as for TR and TO behaviors. In other words, as TR behaviors of the subjects became more frequent, both TO and DB decreased in frequency, and vice-versa.

The results of the Friedman test for differences in academic averages indicated that a chi-square of 44.19, df = 3, was significant (p $<$.01). Post hoc contrasts between average percent of achievement on criterion tests revealed significant differences (p $<$.01) for the following: Conditions One and Two, Conditions One and Four, Conditions Two and Three, and Conditions Three and Four. Thus, the average percent of achievement on the criterion tests was significantly higher in both treatment conditions (Two and Four) than during the baseline conditions (One and Three). Also, using the Wilcoxon Matched-Pairs Test (9), a significant difference (p $<$.01) was found between the pretest and post-test administered during the first treatment condition.

129

DISCUSSION

The lack of significant difference in all categories of class-room behavior between Condition Two and Condition Three as well as between Condition Three and Condition Four is no real cause for alarm. Since Condition Three had a duration of only seven school days and Condition Four was only five school days in length, effects of the use of behavioral objectives, criterion evaluation, and remediation in Condition Two may well have carried over into the other conditions, particularly since many of the subjects had experienced such remarkable improvement in Condition Two.

The significant difference in Time Off Task behaviors which occurred between Condition One and Condition Three (the two baseline conditions) indicated that the children were more willing to continue learning efforts when their teachers were willing to "pay off" for desired behavior. The behaviors which apparently were reinforced by a sense of accomplishment did not decrease significantly following Condition Two. In other words, when the use of behavioral objectives, criterion evaluation, and remediation was eliminated in Condition Three, the subjects continued to exhibit a higher rate of Task Relevant behaviors while their Disruptive Behavior remained essentially the same. Hence, individualization of the instructional process (as opposed to lockstep classroom procedures) apparently served as a strong reinforcer to the subjects.

It should be emphasized that, essentially, for the first time in recent years these subjects had experienced substantial academic

130

progress in Condition Two. Thus, they apparently were more willing to continue to exhibit more Task Relevant behaviors in Condition Three even though their rate of Disruptive Behavior did not change noticeably during that same period. This development also indicated that an increased amount of time spent on learning tasks was not the primary consideration, but that quality of the instructional process was vital (2). For, a comparison of classroom behavior patterns and achievement revealed that achievement levels decreased drastically during Condition Three even though the subjects were spending more time on learning tasks than they did in Condition One. Since the "pay off" (a sense of accomplishment resulting from a modification in instructional technique) in Condition Two apparently caused Task Relevant activity to continue at a more frequent rate in Condition Three than in Condition One, it was assumed that the lack of continued academic gains was not caused by pupil misbehavior (DB) or inattention (TO), but by the change in instructional process.

Of particular interest is the fact that, although no direct manipulation was employed to control the classroom behavior of the disruptive students, TR behaviors increased significantly during treatment conditions. And, as the TR behaviors increased in frequency, TO and DB behaviors decreased.

Participating teachers in the studies referred to in the introduction of this report were given a set of behavioral objectives and were instructed to teach for the achievement of those goals. They selected their own processes. In the present investigation, however, the participating teachers were trained to write and to use behavioral objectives and to employ criterion evaluation and remediation. These controls which were applied to the use of behavioral objectives, criterion evaluation, and remediation vastly improved teacher understanding of the process and provided for uniform manipulation of the independent variable. Consequently, changes in achievement patterns were decisive.

From this investigation it was concluded that the use of behavioral objectives, criterion evaluation, and remediation had a positive effect on the classroom progress of disruptive adolescents. It was found that the participating teachers were able to utilize the process in ways that facilitate learner success.

REFERENCES

1. Baker, E. L. Effects on student achievement of behavioral and non-behavioral objectives. Journal of Experimental Education, 1969, 4, 5-8.

2. Carroll, J. B. A model for school learning. Teachers College Record, 1963, 64, 723-733.

3. Cook, J. M. Learning and retention by informing students of behavioral objectives and their place in the hierarchical learning sequence. United States Department of Health, Education, and Welfare, Office of Education, Research Bureau (November, 1969). Project No. OEC-3-9-090018-0021(010).

4. Engel, R. S. An experimental study of the effects of stated behavioral objectives on achievement in a unit of instruction on negative and rational base systems of numerator. Unpublished Master's thesis, The University of Maryland, College Park, 1968.

5. Hernandez, D. E. Writing Behavioral Objectives. New York: Barnes and Noble, 1971.

6. Jenkins, J. R., and Deno, S. L. Influence of knowledge and type of objectives on subject matter lerarning. Journal of Educational Psychology, 1971, 62, 67-70.

7. Mager, R. F. Preparing Instructional Objectives. New York: Fearon Publishers, Inc., 1962.

8. Marascuilo, L. A. Statistical Methods for Behavioral Science Research. New York: McGraw-Hill Book Company, 1971.

9. Siegel, S. Nonparametric Statistics for the Behavioral Sciences. New York: McGraw-Hill Book Company, 1956.

10. Smith, S. A. The effect of two variables on the achievement of slow learners on a unit in mathematics. Unpublished Master's thesis, The University of Maryland, College Park, 1967.

PATRICIA A. NOLEN
HAROLD P. KUNZELMANN
NORRIS G. HARING

Behavioral Modification in a Junior High Learning Disabilities Classroom

NEW evidence supporting behavioral modification techniques in special education classrooms is reported almost monthly. Those who have extended operant behavioral principles to classroom learning have suggested that complex academic response repertoires may be amenable to a methodology based on a functional analysis of behavior (Bijou and Sturges, 1958; Birnbrauer, Bijou, Wolf, and Kidder, 1966; Staats, Finley, Minke, and Wolf, 1964; Lindsley, 1964; Whitlock, 1966). Whether or not this approach can be applied to situations beyond the short-term clinical or tutorial periods, however, has been the basis for continuing doubt. The heterogeneous enrollments and complex curriculum requirements in most regularly scheduled classrooms have seemed to limit the functionality of operant behavioral analysis to appropriate social behaviors or to short sequences of the program. Preliminary findings from the classrooms of the University of Washington Experimental Education Unit, however, have suggested otherwise. Here ongoing investigations seem to indicate that any limitations imposed upon behavioral analysis at the outset may be premature (Haring and Kunzelmann, 1966; Haring and Lovitt, 1967).

The Experimental Education Unit was organized to provide for the study, assessment, and remediation of educational retardation. Because its research responsibilities are diverse, and because it provides services for teacher training as well as services for exceptional children, the behavioral deviancies of its children span a wider range than is found within the usual special education classrooms. Diagnostic categories represented within any one class are further differentiated as a result of the school unit's involvement in the multidisciplinary Mental Retardation and Child Development Center. Despite the multiplicity and heterogeneity of learning problems, however, each of the unit's five classrooms has provided sufficient evidence in one school term to warrant further investigation of functional behavioral analysis as a classroom teaching and management technique.

The data reported here were taken from the junior high classroom during its first year of operation. Students enrolled in this class were 12 to 16 years in age, with individual achievement levels ranging from preschool to sixth grade. Diagnostic categories and recorded behavioral deviancies covered as wide a span for the one grouping as did the achievement levels. On the referrals, students were listed as "passive-aggressive," "psychotic," "dyslexic," "aphasic," having "generalized mental retardation," being

EXCEPTIONAL CHILDREN, 1967, Vol. 34, pp. 163-168.

"emotionally disturbed," or "neurologically impaired," together with a generally pessimistic prognosis for any long term effect of remedial teaching. Such classifications are not used as criteria for the school unit's enrollment; demonstrated learning deficits are the preferred criteria. With these deficits as primary concerns, the educational diagnostician seeks to identify deficiencies the child may have in content or extent and/or rate of learning within any one or a number of specific academic or social behavioral skill areas. This diagnosis by skill specifics, rather than by physical or psychological deficit, is considered fundamental to the application of behavioral management techniques in the unit's classrooms. It has allowed a much broader view of remedial teaching, which, contrary to the popular notion, has not seemed to neglect the web of dynamic interrelationships posed by such factors as "motivation" or "inadequate self concept." Although these factors have been included within the teaching context, they have been considered as "the ability to respond successfully and effectively." By standards of skill specifics, then, the frequency of accurate academic responses is of primary consideration here.

Initial organization of the classroom entailed an extensive tabulation and compilation of all skills that could be identified within any one academic area. Standard test achievement levels such as "third grade reading comprehension" or "first grade computational ability" simply did not supply the teacher with the precise information on which remediation as behavioral modification could be based. In place of the broad summarization of standardized tests, behavioral definitions of skill sequences were abstracted largely from programed academic curricula for which adequate developmental and field testing data were available. Eventually this detailed outline was expanded to include both teacher designed steps and an increased number of contingencies advocated for optimal learning (Homme, Debaca, Devine, Steinhorst, and Rickert, 1963). An interesting outcome of the analysis was the finding that, for most learners, an optimal program requires less of the former and more of the latter.

It is not new to note that present knowledge allows only an approximation of the structure of any one content area. Within these limitations, an attempt was made to define as many steps in a particular learning sequence as could be identified. It is believed that this may be necessary before attempting to order classroom learning situations for the employment of behavioral modification techniques.

Observers invariably made remarks about the lengthy and detailed skill sequence sheets (University of Washington College of Education, 1966), saying that although the idea was praiseworthy, a teacher could not possibly know every child's attainment or exact direction of skills at any one time. Those who had the opportunity to test this assumption, however, found that the unit's teachers did in fact know a child's skills and would use and often revise these skill outlines. In the junior high class, for example, a student was not merely "working on multiplication," he was working with multiplication of whole numbers defined in terms of repeated addition or reconstructing multiplication equations with a missing product or missing factor in combinations through 5 x 9 or studying in another area which had been analyzed with similar detail. Answers also referred to comparative rates of performance, computed not between students but between any two performances of the same student.

Program Stimuli

Once both skill sequences and the student's functioning at some point in the sequence were identified, the designation of the program was no simple task of matching student and workbook at some certain grade level. On the contrary, completely individual programs were organized. These were built largely from commercially programed materials together with selections from traditional texts and workbooks. Often the linear progression was achieved only with the design of supplements programed to overcome deficits in the sequence. During the second year of operation, while refinements in programing continued, individualization of instruction for a student became less of a problem than individualization of a particular content area. From these initial programs, preliminary task analyses of specific and generic teaching points were outlined in terms of their distribution and interrelation.

Reinforcement Contingencies

Although the stimulus program (an attempt to define and arrange academic responses) played an important role in the organization of an operant classroom, reinforcement contingencies were the major concern. Two principles guided the exploration of reinforcement contingencies in the unit's classrooms: the first, what is known as "high probability behavior," is a concept well substantiated by the work of Premack (1965) and Homme et al. (1963). This behavior occurs at a high rate prior to educational or clinical intervention; it consists of those things the student most often chooses to do, providing a source for "natural" consequences for the manipulation and acceleration of low probability behavior; the second requirement was that both high probability behavior and any other consequences assumed to be "secondary reinforcers" were ultimately acceptable in a traditionally organized classroom. This second principle precluded at the outset the use of money, candy, or trinkets, the "consumable/manipulatable" classifications of the laboratories (Bijou and Sturges, 1958). Further, the singular use of social approval as a durable reinforcing consequence did not seem to offer the initial control needed for programing the multiple contingencies of a group situation. Moreover, it did not seem that classroom management could be optimally based on the assumption that social approval was a reinforcer for those adolescents with a history of school and interpersonal failure (Bijou and Baer, 1966).

In an attempt to standardize the number of stimuli presupposed to be "natural" consequences of high strength behavior, the teacher allotted points for the child's successful completion of each of a number of gradually lengthening academic tasks. A running record of these points was kept at each child's desk, and these points were negotiable at any time for play periods analogous to school recesses or for a variety of enrichment or practical studies in the public schools (Haring and Kunzelmann, 1966). The junior high students' most preferred choices for contingent high strength behavior centered on handicrafts, typing, woodworking, organized games, or science units. These choices were somewhat surprising to the teaching staff, who had made an effort to supply what are considered culturally determined "reinforcers" for adolescents by extending the available consequences to include slot cars, models, popular recordings, and teen magazines, on the assumption that such choices would be replaced only by gradually shaping preferences for the more traditional school activities.

Data Collection

Unlike procedures used in the majority of operant studies, the experimenter-teacher did not have the exclusive function of establishing individual behavioral baselines. Using service as one of the operational criteria, baseline or "operant level" was determined by (a) anecdotal records and achievement test scores from the student's school records prior to enrollment in the unit, and (b) rate of daily academic responses recorded on the first day of enrollment. It seemed advisable to begin the teaching method on the first day, with concomitant manipulation of high and low strength behaviors not only from a first day service viewpoint but also due to the ease of its application to a group admitting new members during the school year. The data were recorded in terms of both subject matters and total academic responses for each student over a period of 100 days.

Indications

The resulting data from the first year's efforts at organizing a special education classroom on a behavioral basis are shown in Figure 1. These records include only reading and arithmetic responses, excepting the modification of social behaviors which accompanied remedial skill instruction. Throughout the 24 week instructional period, an effort was made to define "academic response" individually for each student and for each particular subject area. In the initial stages of reading, for example, the correct association of a letter shape with a sound was an adequate response for the application of negotiable consequences. Later, however, once the association had been cued, prompted, and practiced without prompts, the single element became part of a chain included in the definition of a succeeding response. In other words, sound-symbol relationships, phonic blending and sight words, and eventually oral reading of a complete sentence were all progressively defined as a single response for recording purposes and for consequence application.

In like manner, arithmetical functioning was ordered in successive stages which began with the manipulation of actual concrete physical quantities, followed by the manipulation of physical representations, then abstract repre-

FIGURE 1. Cumulative Academic Record

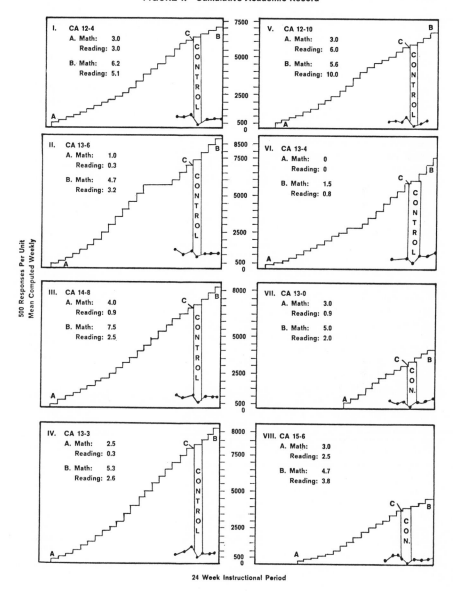

sentations prior to any association of numerals with numbers or symbols with operations. As in reading, antecedent steps in any arithmetical sequence were considered chained in subsequent, more complex responses.

Each graph in Figure 1 represents one student's weekly cumulative record of frequency of correct academic responses in reading and mathematics during that part of the instructional period in which he was enrolled. After a high rate of responding had been established, the procedure was altered in an attempt to isolate the function of contingent delivery of the points negotiable for high strength activities. During this control period, four time allotments for high strength activities were scheduled daily for each student. Unlike the organization of the school day prior and subsequent to the control period, the high strength activities at this time were contingent neither upon accuracy nor on rate of responding. In this way, the free time followed not as a consequence upon completion of work but upon mere passage of time. Point C on each record identifies the cumulative responses during this interval of reversal. A graph of the drop in the mean number of responses during the five day control period and the subsequent rise during reinstatement of contingencies is displayed at the base of each record.

Notations accompanying response records of eight of the junior high students show beginning achievement levels on the basis of referral reports (A), and achievement levels at the close of the first instructional period of approximately 100 days (B). Even though the programs were based largely on a structural linguistic approach in reading and the "new" mathematics process in arithmetic, terminal levels have been determined on the basis of scores on the Metropolitan Achievement Tests, an instrument which does not always reflect the newer instructional emphasis on process as well as product.

While the original records note any absences from the classroom during the school day as a result of illness, clinic visits, or scheduled appointments with any of the unit's supporting services, no compensations for resulting discrepancies in response frequencies have been included. Nor do these records show one of the most welcome by-products of the use of high strength activities to reinforce a low entering

level of responding. Seldom if ever did observers to the classroom fail to note the personal pride in achievement evidenced verbally by students. Surprisingly, this came not only as a result of a more generous allotment for minimal functioning in a new skill sequence, but also for the gradual reduction in allotment of points for review work of an increasingly complex and time consuming nature.

Not included in this report is a study of the modification of inappropriate classroom social behavior as the primary goal for a 13 year old male prior to an analysis of subject matter functioning. Whereas this particular student was withdrawn by parental request, it must also be noted that his reinstatement was requested by the parent within a short time.

Conclusion

The acceleration of academic response rates of adolescent students with learning disorders participating in this limited application of functional behavioral analysis to academic performance has stimulated wide interest among personnel in surrounding school districts. Reports indicate that similar behavioral management techniques are either under consideration or in practice at this time. Followup studies of three of the students who have been transferred from this classroom show that, although the acceleration of their rates to peaks of 500 or more responses per day have not been maintained under traditional classroom contingency arrangements, in each case levels of achievement have been maintained and response rates have exceeded those of other members of the transfer classrooms. For those students who were maintained for a second teaching session at the unit, a nine week summer vacation did not interrupt the individual response patterns or rates of acceleration.

In addition, the records from the junior high teacher's parental conferences show that there have been changes in the verbal content of the conferences which have accompanied the increases in individual response rates. The most consistent change recorded is a decrease in parental requests for such conferences on the basis of a student's functioning and an increase in parental requests for detailed explanations of the techniques of classroom management.

As a result of such parental demands, study groups for parental education have been planned for those parents asking to participate. A decrease in parental requests for conferences concerning academic progress, and an increase in their requests for management information, seem to indicate that the behavioral changes of the students are, in fact, generalizing to situations other than the controlled environment of the classroom.

References

Bijou, S. W., and Baer, D. M. Operant methods in child behavior and development. In W. K. Honig (Editor), *Operant behavior*. New York: Appleton-Century-Crofts, 1966. Pp. 778-782.

Bijou, S. W., and Sturges, P. T. Positive reinforcers for experimental studies with children—consumables and manipulables. *Child Development*, 1958, 30, 151-170.

Birnbrauer, J. S., Bijou, S. W., Wolf, M. M., and Kidder, J. D. Programmed instruction in the classroom. In L. P. Ullman and L. Krasner (Editors), *Case studies in behavior modification*. New York: Holt, Rinehart and Winston, 1966. Pp. 358-366.

University of Washington College of Education. *Experimental Education Unit mathematics skill sequence sheet*. Seattle, Washington: Author, 1966.

Haring, N. G., and Kunzelmann, H. P. Finer focus of therapeutic behavior management. In J. Hellmuth (Editor), *Educational therapy*. Seattle, Washington: Special Child Publications, 1966. Pp. 225-251.

Haring, N. G., and Lovitt, T. C. Operant methodology and educational technology in special education. In N. G. Haring and R. L. Schiefulbusch (Editors), *Methods in special education*. New York: McGraw-Hill, 1967. Pp. 12-48.

Homme, L., Debaca, P., Devine, J., Steinhorst, R., and Rickert, E. Use of the Premack principle in controlling the behavior of nursery school children. *Journal of Experimental Analysis of Behavior*, 1963, 6, 544.

Lindsley, O. R. Direct measurement and prosthesis of retarded behavior. *Journal of Education*, 1964, 147, 62-81.

Premack, D. Reinforcement theory. In D. Levine (Editor), *Nebraska symposium on motivation*. Lincoln, Nebraska: University of Nebraska Press, 1965. Pp. 123-189.

Staats, A. W., Finley, J. R., Minke, K. A., and Wolf, M. Reinforcement variables in the control of unit reading response. *Journal of the Experimental Analysis of Behavior*, 1964, 7, 139-149.

Whitlock, Sister Carolyn. Note on reading acquisition: an extension of laboratory principles. *Journal of Experimental Child Psychology*, 1966, 3, 83-85.

The Influence of Massive Rewards on Reading Achievement in Potential Urban School Dropouts

CARL A. CLARK

HERBERT J. WALBERG

Most theories of learning emphasize reinforcement as an important determinant of behavior, and yet no randomized, controlled experiments have been done in school classrooms (Parton and Ross, 1965). This study reports an investigation of this problem in an after-school reading program for children in the Chicago Public Schools.[2] The experiment took place in the south side of the innercity, an area populated by rural, Negro migrants from Alabama, Georgia, and Mississippi and their first and second generations. The neighborhood is characterized by low standards of living and high rates of social pathology: unemployment, crime, and school attrition. Nationally-standardized achievement tests of children in this part of the city show that they are from one to four years behind typical levels of children in the same age and grade. One can imagine—and confirm by observation—that for these children, school work is frustrating and negatively reinforcing. The object of this study was to make the reinforcement positive with massive verbal rewards given by the teacher and tallied by each child, and to observe its effect on reading achievement.

There were three problems faced in conducting this experiment. The first had to do with the random assignment of pupils to experi-

AMERICAN EDUCATION RESEARCH JOURNAL, 1968, Vol. 5, pp. 305-310.

mental and control conditions necessary for statistical tests. If there is random assignment within classrooms, there is the problem of interaction between experimental and control subjects. If intact classes are assigned to experimental and control conditions, there is the problem of non-chance differences, and there are usually not enough classes available for an adequate "groups within treatments" or "random replications" design (Lindquist, 1953). Fortunately, for our experiment, the administrators and teachers cooperated insofar as to enable random assignment of pupils to class as well as classes to experimental and control conditions.[1]

The second problem was the control and measurement of rewards. For the present study we used individual cards given daily to each pupil, each card containing numbered squares the pupil could circle when rewarded and told to do so by the teacher. The basic reason for the use of the cards was not to introduce a special reward system, but to have a means of quantifying the number of rewards received by each pupil. Other systems are possible, one being to have observers record the rewards; but this system involves an intrusion into the normal classroom situation, and could have its own effect, hard to assess. Another way is to have the teacher record the rewards given to each pupil, but this method takes a good deal of the teacher's time and attention from his work.

With the card system used, the cards could be collected at the end of the period and the number of rewards for each pupil tallied. Of course this system is not foolproof either. a pupil could mark his card when he is not receiving rewards. In order to help control for this possibility, the pupils were given special blue pencils with blue-colored "leads" that they were to pick up and use only when, after being praised, they were told to circle a number. Numbers circled with their ordinary pencils would not count, and it would be fairly obvious if a pupil picked up and used the special blue pencil —obvious to the teacher and to the other pupils.

A special problem with the use of the blue pencil and card reward recording system was the possible "gadget effect." So far as this effect in itself contributed a reward there was not much of a problem since we were more concerned with the fact of reward than the

1. The writers wish to thank Louise Dougherty and Alfred Rudd for administrative support, the cooperating teachers for their participation, and Ina Turner for clerical assistance.

type of reward. We did two things, however, to lessen and to control for a "gadget effect" and for the so-called "Hawthorne effect." One was to have both the experimental and control groups use the cards for tallying rewards, and the other was to have both groups go through a control period of several sessions, during which time the novelty effect could wear off.

Finally, there was the problem of measuring the effect of rewards on the dependent variable, which was reading achievement in this experiment. When pre and post test scores are used over a comparatively short time interval, several problems are introduced into the analysis: there are the effects of regression toward the mean, item memory practice, and others which obscure the results. It was decided, therefore, that the main analysis would be based on a single reading test given at the end of the experiment. Some control over initial individual differences would be attained by using IQ as a control variable in an analysis of covariance procedure.

METHOD

Subjects

The 110 children in the experiment were from 10 to 13 years of age and from one to four years behind in their school work. For these reasons they were considered potential dropouts and were assigned on a random basis to nine classes in an after-school remedial reading program with from 10 to 15 children in each class.

Procedure

At the beginning of the experiment all the teachers and children were asked to follow the same instructions. Each child received the especially prepared tally card which we have described, and the teachers were asked to distribute the praise rewards so that each child, even the very slow ones, would get at least several each day. After the teacher made a rewarding remark, she directed the rewarded child to make a tally mark on his card on a list of numbers, from 1 to 50. The child made the marks sequentially, beginning with number one. At the end of the class session he wrote down the total number of tally marks (therefore of rewards) he had received for the day. The teachers checked the card markings for accuracy, and sent the cards to the experimenters after each class.

After six sessions the reward rates per child and per teacher appeared to stabilize, and the five teachers (randomly determined) of the experimental groups were confidentially asked to double or triple the number of rewards while the four teachers of the control groups were asked to "keep up the good work." After these requests were made, large increments appeared in the number of tally marks on cards for the experimental group while the numbers for the control group remained at approximately the same levels.

At the end of the second three week period, the 62 children in the experimental groups and the 48 in the control groups took the Science Research Associates Reading Test, Intermediate Form. The total raw scores only were used in the analyses.

RESULTS

The mean for the experimental groups was 31.62, with a standard deviation of 7.43, and the mean for the control groups was 26.86, with a standard deviation of 8.60. The analysis of variance for the unadjusted raw scores produced an F-ratio of 9.52 (p less than 1 percent; see Table 1). In the covariance analysis with Kuhlman-Anderson IQs as the control variable, the F-ratio was 7.90 (p less than 1 percent). This F-ratio is smaller than the one for unadjusted

TABLE 1

Analyses of Variance and Covariance for SRA Reading and K-A Intelligence Test Scores

Scores	Sum of Squares	df	Mean Squares	F-Ratio
SRA Reading				
Between	616.82	1	616.82	9.52*
Within	6994.45	108	64.76	
Total	7611.27	109		
K-A Intelligence				
Between	176.55	1	176.55	1.84
Within	10,337.41	108	95.72	
Total	10,513.96	109		
Adjusted SRA**				
Between	488.40	1	488.40	7.90*
Within	6614.43	107	61.82	
Total	7102.83	108		

* Significant at the 1 percent level.
** The correlation between the SRA and the KA was .26.

143

scores, even though the error mean square is smaller, because the between treatments mean square for adjusted scores was only slightly lower. The mean IQ for the experimental group, 92.05, was slightly but not significantly higher than the control group mean, 90.73.

DISCUSSION

The hypothesis was strongly supported: children who were massively rewarded scored significantly higher on a standardized reading test. Although the idea that reinforcement enhances learning has long been known in the field of psychology, it seemed revolutionary to the teachers and children in this experiment. It is not enough apparently, simply to instruct student teachers or regular teachers to use rewards to control behavior. The use of a reward tally card which focused the attention of the teacher and the child on the rewards seemed much more convincing. The request to distribute the rewards to insure that each child got at least a few each time also had a beneficial effect.

Some logical steps follow from this study. One would examine the effects of distinct reward schedules (ratio and interval); the ones used in this study were mixed. Another would determine the long term efficacy of massive rewards. One interesting hypothesis is that it is the increase differential across time that increases learning rather than continuous high rates which may lead to satiation. A third possible avenue of research would be to investigate the validity of these findings across children grouped by age, socioeconomic class, sex, school class and other relevant factors.

Parton and Ross (1965) in a review of research on social reinforcement of children's motor behavior have criticized the methods of previous studies in this area particularly with regard to the common omission of the control group. Methodologically, we have shown here that it is possible to randomly assign children to experimental and control groups in school classrooms, to randomly administer (with the class as the unit) an experimental treatment (massive verbal rewards) in measured amounts (tallied on cards by the pupils themselves), and to demonstrate significant differences between groups on a measure of achievement (a standardized reading test). Theoretically, we have confirmed the hypothesis from reinforcement theories of learning that verbal rewards have efficacy in the control of operant behavior in human subjects. And lastly, from a practical point of view, we have shown in an actual educational setting, that the teacher's increased use of verbal praise has a positive effect on the scholastic learning of children who are potential dropouts from inner-city schools.

REFERENCES

LINDQUIST, E. F. *Design and Analysis of Experiments in Psychology and Education.* Boston: Houghton Mifflin, 1953.

PARTON, David A., & ROSS, Allan O. "Social Reinforcement of Children's Motor Behavior: a Review." *Psychological Bulletin* 64:65-73; 1965.

SECTION FIVE

APPLICATIONS TO SOCIAL PROBLEMS

When one surveys the problems of our society, e.g., racist behaviors, environmental pollution, and over-population, he naturally longs for an institution which could solve those problems. We feel that the school presently offers more hope for dealing with societal problems than any of our current institutions. At least, no other insitution can match the amount of time the school has to effect change in the lives of children.

If the school is to deal with society's problems, how? Since this book is based on the premise that operant procedures are highly effective educational tools, we might expect such techniques to offer great promise for improving the state of society. Unfortunately, practically no research studies have focused directly on this possibility. Two studies (Burgess, Clark, and Hendee, 1971; Williams, Cormier, Sapp, and Andrews, 1971) are unique in that they do attempt to demonstrate how operant procedures can be used in improving environmental pollution and interaction among racial groups. We hope that these studies will prove to be precursors of considerable operant research dealing with critical social problems.

THE UTILITY OF BEHAVIOR MANAGEMENT TECHNIQUES IN CHANGING INTERRACIAL BEHAVIORS

Department of Educational Psychology, The University of Tennessee

ROBERT L. WILLIAMS, WILLIAM H. CORMIER, GARY L. SAPP,
AND HENRY B. ANDREWS

A. INTRODUCTION

Recently, behavior management techniques have been applied to quite an array of classroom behaviors (4, 5, 6). Such procedures as contingent teacher attention, peer reinforcement, and role modeling have been used successfully to alter task relevant and disruptive classroom behavior. One area that has been relatively untouched in behavior modification studies is biracial interaction. Can the extent to which black and white students interact with each other be altered via systematic social reinforcement?

The vigorous attempts of the U.S. Department of Health, Education, and Welfare (HEW) and the federal courts to achieve a balanced distribution of blacks and whites in public school systems is apparently based on the premise that physical desegregation will lead to social integration. However, there is little empirical evidence to corroborate this assumption. Several studies indicate that social integration is by no means an inevitable result of physical desegregation (1, 2, 3, 7, 8). Simply putting blacks and whites together does not assure that they will interact with each other or develop increased affinity for each other.

The present study is based on the premise that the achievement of social integration between blacks and whites must be deliberately planned for within the school setting. Otherwise, social integration is not likely to occur. The current investigation appraised the efficacy of five behavior management procedures, contingent teacher reinforcement, peer reinforcement, role modeling, group reinforcement counseling, and a control condition, in altering interracial behaviors.

JOURNAL OF PSYCHOLOGY, 1971, Vol. 77, pp. 127-138.

B. METHOD

1. *Subjects*

The junior high school used in this study was located in a metropolitan area of Tennessee. At the time of the study the school was drawing students from (*a*) an all-black section of the city, (*b*) an all-white Ku Klux Klan (KKK) type neighborhood, and (*c*) a desegregated housing project. Prior to 1965 the school was all-white. In 1965, the school's first year of desegregation, 20 percent of the student body was black. For the next three years the school had a 50-50% racial balance. In 1969-1970, when the study was conducted, the racial distribution was 60% blacks and 40% whites. Theoretically, with this kind of racial balance a student has about as much opportunity to interact with the opposite race as with his own race. However, sociometric data collected during the 1968-1969 school year indicated that the school was sharply polarized with respect to race (8).

The subjects were selected from five classes which had racially balanced enrollments (near 50-50%). In each class, six black racial isolates and six white isolates were identified via sociometric data as follows. Students in each class were administered eight social situations dealing with routine classroom activity, informal play activity outside the classroom, inviting friends to their home, sponsored school activity within the community milieu, formal extracurricular activity at school, seating patterns for meals at school, intellectually demanding activity at school, and school-related social functions. For each situation the students were asked to identify the three students from their class with whom they would most like to share the experience and the three students with whom they would least like to share the experience.

Students who gave and received the *lowest* number of biracial choices, while giving and receiving the *highest* number of biracial rejections, were identified as racial isolates. A total racial isolation score based on all eight situations was computed for each student by adding biracial choices given and received and subtracting from that total biracial rejections given and received. Since very few biracial choices were given and a great many biracial rejections were given, the total racial isolation score was negative for most students. However, students obtaining the most negative scores in each class were identified as racial isolates.

To corroborate the premise that the students identified as biracial isolates were significantly more isolated than other members of the class, a comparison was made between the isolates' scores and those of 12 other students selected randomly from the remaining class members. Analysis of variance indicated that the isolates' scores were significantly ($p < .0001$) more negative than the nonisolates scores at the beginning of the study. Isolates in the five treatment groups did not differ significantly from each other at the outset of the study. Posttreatment assessment indicated that the isolates had become significantly ($p < .0001$) less negative in their total racial isolation scores, whereas the nonisolates had become slightly more negative.

2. *Treatments*

Although individual isolates were not randomly assigned to treatments, the treatment conditions were randomly assigned to the five classes. Therefore, the probability that an isolate would wind up in a particular treatment condition was the same as for any other isolate. Treatment implementation was initiated immediately after the Christmas holidays and continued through May 15. Implementation of treatments was monitored by observers from the University of Tennessee. With the exception of the teacher reinforcement condition, each treatment and control group was observed four periods a day for the duration of the treatment. Since only three teachers participated in the teacher reinforcement treatment, this group was observed just for those three periods.

a. Teacher Reinforcement. The Ss selected for this treatment condition were 12 seventh graders, six black (five boys and one girl) and six white (three boys and three girls) students. Two female teachers (one black and one white) and a white male teacher were the sources of social reinforcement for the isolates. This treatment was based on the assumption that the most important social relationship in the classroom is that between a student and his teacher. The Es felt that a student's relationship with his teacher could have a decisive impact on his behavior toward other students, particularly members of the opposite race. Previous observation of teacher behavior had indicated that most junior high school teachers criticize students much more frequently than they praise them. It is likely that this criticism produces considerable hostility toward the teacher, and when students are not allowed to express that hostility directly, they seek other targets—e.g., members of the opposite race—for their hostility. It was hypothesized, therefore, that reinforcing (e.g., praising, touching, listening to) students would improve the teacher-student relationship and, consequently, the student-student relationship in the classroom.

Teacher training consisted of several meetings with the three teachers to acquaint them with the principles of social reinforcement, the treatment instructions on reinforcing appropriate behavior and ignoring inappropriate behavior, and examples of the treatment procedures demonstrated on video tape.

After the treatment conditions were introduced, each teacher was video-taped in his class. Teachers then viewed their own video tapes and the taped sequences of the other teachers. The next phase of training consisted of the *E*s teaching the treatment classes for one day and the teachers recording the frequency and kind of social attention the *E*s gave to each *S*.

Throughout treatment implementation, observers recorded the frequency and type of teacher attention (verbal praise, smiles, touch, or any other social interaction) to appropriate *S* behavior and to inappropriate *S* behavior. With this information, the *E*s provided feedback to each teacher concerning his effectiveness in reinforcing the isolates. During treatment the amount of attention given appropriate student behavior was several times as great as attention to inappropriate behavior. It was not uncommon for a treatment teacher to attend to appropriate behavior of the isolates 50 times or more during a class session, while attending to inappropriate behavior no more than once or twice. One of three teachers consistently had more than 60 instances of attending to appropriate isolate behavior and no instances of attending to inappropriate behavior.

b. Peer Reinforcement. The *S*s selected for the peer reinforcement condition were 12 seventh graders, six blacks (four males and two females) and six whites (four males and two females). Three black and three white students who gave and received the highest number of biracial choices in the class, who received a high number of choices from within their own race, and who gave and received few biracial rejections served as the peer reinforcers for the racial isolates. The reinforcers were trained via video-taped demonstrations and role play to attend to (praise, smile, touch, talk, listen) appropriate behavior emitted by the isolates and ignore inappropriate behavior.

The class participating in this part of the study was together for four periods a day. Each reinforcer was assigned an isolate to work with each period. Assignments were made on a rotating basis so that each reinforcer worked with each isolate several times during the course of the treatment. Students selected as isolates were never told they were "isolates" nor was the purpose of the study discussed with them. Furthermore, students selected as peer reinforcers were never told that their targets were "racial isolates."

Throughout the treatment, observers recorded the type and frequency of interaction between the reinforcers and the isolates. Each reinforcer was observed for two class periods a day. Observers were instructed to approve verbally peer reinforcers for desirable reinforcement behavior. In addition, peer reinforcers were given tangible rewards (mainly edibles) once a week for appropriate interaction with isolates. Throughout treatment, most reinforcers exhibited a higher frequency of intraracial interaction than biracial. The high point of biracial interaction between reinforcers and isolates was obtained after about one month of treatment.

The peer reinforcement treatment was based on the rationale that a major reason why students are racial isolates is because of the dearth of positive reinforcement received from members of the opposite race. If a student consistently receives reinforcement from members of the other race, it is likely he will develop a greater affinity for that race. Simply stated, a person will not continue to dislike and avoid individuals who are being nice to him.

c. Role Modeling. The six black (four males, two females) and six white (five males, one female) isolates who served as *S*s for the role modeling treatment were in the eighth grade. The role models were students who gave and received the highest number of biracial choices, received a high number of choices from their own race, and concomitantly gave and received the lowest number of biracial rejections. Biracial triads (problem solving groups) comprised of an isolate *(I)*, a role model *(RM)* of the *I*'s race and a high status model *(HSM)* of the opposite race were the major vehicles of treatment administration. Triads were conducted on a daily basis in each of the four classes attended by the isolates and models. Triad members and group activities were scheduled so that each *I* worked in a triad once every three class days. Triad members engaged in a variety of tasks ranging from working on assigned subject matter to constructing model cars, playing word games, conducting experiments in science, working on class reports and discussing problems in school. Each *RM* and *HSM* served in one triad per day. The behavior of each *RM* and *HSM* was observed for the duration of a triadic session.

A crucial objective in this treatment was the achievement of appropriate interaction between *(a)* the *RM* and the *HSM* and *(b)* the two models and the *I*. To attain this objective, the students functioning as models were trained to interact appropriately with other students. These appropriate behaviors consisted of talking to members of the opposite race in the triad, praising the other group members, listening attentively to members of the opposite race in the triad, and minimizing criticism of other triad members.

Training procedures consisted of having models read a previously prepared script, engage in spontaneous role playing, and view video tapes demonstrating treatment techniques. Throughout the study an *E* met with the *RM*s and *HSM*s once a week to give them feedback concerning the appropriateness of their behavior (based on the observers' report) and to dispense various tangible rewards. In addition, teachers were instructed to reinforce the triad members for working together as a group.

The rationale for the role modeling treatment was based on the Bandura and Walters' role modeling paradigm. Simply stated, the role modeling paradigm suggests that human beings learn to behave as they observe others behaving. However, a child is more likely to imitate a model that he perceives as being similar to himself than one he perceives as dissimilar. Children are also more likely to imitate a model they view as having some degree of status and one who is reinforced for the behavior in question. The role modeling treatment in the current study attempted to incorporate these basic components of the Bandura and Walters' role modeling paradigm.

d. Group Process. The 12 isolates used in this treatment condition were selected from a section of the eighth grade. The *S*s were divided into two small groups with three white and three black students in each group. The same *E* acted as leader for both groups. Each group met for one hour each week to discuss problems related to their school and community. All group sessions were conducted outside the classroom. Most of the early group discussions dealt with teacher-student conflicts, but the *E* suggested several topics dealing with racial issues—e.g., black-white dating, "gang" conflicts between blacks and whites, racial feelings within the group, and parental racial prejudice—which were discussed in the later meetings.

In both groups the *E* provided social reinforcement for any *S* response judged to be appropriate to the group process. Social reinforcement for relatively positive intraracial interaction usually consisted of a smile or head-nod with a concomitant statement of "Good," or "I like what you said." Positive interracial interaction was followed by more extensive social reinforcement, usually consisting of a verbal summarization of the *S*'s remark plus a verbal indication that the opposite race group member had agreed with what had been said.

The group process treatment was based on the assumption that a candid exchange of feelings between blacks and whites may be indispensable to achieving racial harmony. However, open expression of feelings could lead to greater disharmony unless negative feelings are somehow weakened in intensity and positive feelings strengthened. The group leader attempted to accomplish this objective by selective reinforcement of positive interracial interaction.

Although all group sessions were conducted outside the classroom, this treatment group received the same number of in-class observations during treatment implementation as the other treatment groups.

e. Control. Six black (one male, five females) and six white (four males, two females) isolates from a section of the seventh grade served as control *S*s. They received the same number of in-class observations as other treatment groups, but no treatment was employed with them.

3. *Dependent Variables*

Pre- and posttreatment assessments were made for two major types of variables: (*a*) sociometric choices and rejections, and (*b*) behavioral interaction between blacks and whites. The pretreatment dependent measures were collected during the latter part of November, 1969, and the posttreatment measures during the latter part of May, 1970.

a. Sociometric indices. The eight social situations used to select isolates, peer reinforcers, and role models were employed in the pre- and posttreatment assessment of sociometric choices and rejections. For each situation, the students were asked to identify three other students with whom they would like to share the experience and three with whom they would not like to share the experience. Choices and rejections were summed across the eight situations to yield the following dependent measures: (*a*) number of biracial choices given, (*b*) number of biracial choices received, (*c*) number of mutual biracial choices, (*d*) number of biracial rejections given, and (*e*) number of biracial rejections received. A total racial isolation score was computed for each subject by adding number of biracial choices given and received and subtracting from that total biracial rejections given and received.

b. Behavioral interaction. The more important dependent variable in the study was actual interaction between blacks and whites in a classroom setting. During the one week of pretreatment assessment and the one week of posttreatment assessment, four teachers in each treatment group concluded the formal lesson activity in the treatment classes 15 minutes before the end of the period. The students were told they could have the rest of the period to move around the room and talk with whomever they wished. Therefore, each treatment class experienced 60 minutes of free interaction time each day of pre- and posttreatment assessment. During this free time, isolates were observed with respect to their interaction with members of the opposite race. Because of a plurality of observers in some classes, each group of isolates was observed for a total of 105 minutes per day and each isolate close to 10 minutes per day.

The observers classified the isolates' behavior into three major categories: biracial verbal interaction, biracial nonverbal interaction, and none of the above (mainly included intraracial interaction). Biracial verbal interaction consisted of talking or listening to a member of the other race and nonverbal interaction of a physical gesture—e.g., hand waving, winking, smiling—directed toward a member of the other race.

In recording behavior, the observers used rating sheets delineated into five-second time intervals. At the end of each five-second time interval the observer recorded the major behavior emitted by his isolate during the interval. Each observer observed a single isolate for five minutes at a time. Therefore, during five minutes of observation, the observer recorded 60 behavioral incidents. The observer was kept abreast of the time via an audio tape calibrated in five-second time intervals. Ear plugs were used in monitoring the tapes.

Observer training consisted of rating video-taped segments of classroom biracial interaction. Each observer continued to rate behavior until he achieved at least 80% agreement with the trainer (one of the Es). Percentage of agreement was computed by dividing the number of agreements by number of agreements plus disagreements.

C. Results

The effects of specific treatments on biracial measures were established via a three-dimensional mixed, analysis of variance design. The design included two between variables, race (black, white) and treatment (teacher reinforcement, peer reinforcement, role modeling, group process, control), and one within variable(pretreatment, posttreatment).

1. *Sociometric Indices*

The major index of biracial sociometric relationships was the total racial isolation score. Analysis of results revealed a pre-post main effect positive change for all groups on this variable. The Group Process and Role Modeling isolates made the greatest gains and the Control group the least gain. However, differences between groups in amount of gain were not statistically significant. Analysis of a significant race by time (pre-post) interaction indicated that whites made significantly greater gains than blacks on the total racial isolation variable. Mean racial isolation scores for all groups at the pre- and posttreatment levels are included in Table 1.

Most of the pre-post differences in total racial isolation scores can be accounted for by decrements in number of biracial rejections given and received. The five treatment groups yielded a pre-post main effect reduction ($p < .001$) on both variables. The Group Process and Role Modeling Ss yielded the greatest reduction in number of rejections given, whereas the Control Group made the least reduction. On rejections received, the Group Process Ss yielded the greatest decrement and the Peer Reinforcement and Control groups the least decrement. None of these differences between groups in amount of decrease was statistically significant. Analysis of a race $\times$ treatment $\times$ time interaction indicated that whites in the Peer Reinforcement and Role Modeling

155

TABLE 1
GROUP MEANS FOR TOTAL RACIAL ISOLATION SCORES

Treatment group[b]	Pre Racial means	Pre Group means	Post Racial means	Post Group means	Differences[a] Pre-post differences in racial means	Pre-post differences in group means
I-B	—25.167		—18.833		6.334	
I-W	—29.333	—27.250	—21.167	—20.000	8.166	7.250
II-B	—26.833		—25.667		1.166	
II-W	—43.000	—34.917	—36.167	—30.917	6.833	4.000
III-B	—28.500		—21.500		7.000	
III-W	—25.333	—26.917	—16.667	—19.083	8.666	7.834
IV-B	—26.667		—17.500		9.167	
IV-W	—30.167	—28.417	— 3.000	—10.250	27.167	18.167
V-B	—27.167		—28.167		—1.000	
V-W	—27.667	—27.417	— 4.000	—16.083	23.667	11.334

[a] Since all mean scores are negative, a decrease from pre- to post-treatment is considered a positive change and an increase a negative change.

[b] Treatment groups: I-B = Peer reinforcement-Black; I-W = Peer reinforcement-White; II-B = Control-Black; II-W = Control-White; III-B = Teacher reinforcement-Black; III-W = Teacher reinforcement-White; IV-B = Group process-Black; IV-W = Group process-White; V-B = Role modeling-Black; V-W = Role modeling-White.

groups decreased significantly more than blacks with respect to biracial rejections given. Biracial choices given, biracial choices received, and mutual biracial choices remained essentially unchanged from pre- to posttreatment assessment. The only significant finding of major relevance on these variables was an $A \times B \times C$ interaction for biracial choices given. Analysis of this interaction indicated that blacks in the Group Process condition gained significantly from pre- to post, but that whites did not.

2. Behavioral Interaction

In the analysis of biracial behavior, the verbal and nonverbal biracial behavioral categories were combined. A time main effect indicated that all groups in combination increased significantly ($p = .03$) from pre- to post-treatment. Of these groups, the Peer Reinforcement and Teacher Reinforcement groups made the most substantial gains and the Control Group the least gain. Again, differences in amount of gain were not significant. Despite gains on these measures by some groups, the percentage of biracial behavior remained far below the percentage of intraracial behavior.

D. DISCUSSION

Two factors in the current study make it hazardous to affirm the superiority of any one treatment in changing interracial measures. One factor was the failure to obtain a significant treatment by time interaction. The significant pre-post main effect on both major dependent variables, in combination with nonsignificant treatment $\times$ time interactions, indicates that the groups did not differ in amount of gain at the .05 probability level. A second factor delimiting the generalizability of the findings was the lack of consistency in the absolute differences that were obtained. On both the behavioral interaction and total racial isolation indices, the Control group yielded the least positive changes of any treatment group. Beyond that, there is little consistency in the group differences. For example, the Peer Reinforcement group made the greatest gains on behavioral interaction, but ranked fourth on total racial isolation changes. In contrast, the Group Process Ss ranked first on sociometric changes and fourth on behavioral interaction changes.

One explanation for these differences in treatment effects is that the Peer Reinforcement program focused on positive behavioral interaction between isolates and members of the other race and the Group Process experience emphasized discussion of feelings about members of the other race. The latter approach would be more likely to produce changes in feelings and the former changes in behavior. In the current study, the confidential sociometric responses most likely provided the most sensitive measure of covert feelings, and assessment of biracial interaction provided a direct measure of behavior.

There are several factors which may have militated against more positive results in the study. One is a satiation effect. It is the feeling of the Es that the highest point of biracial interaction would probably have been obtained near the midpoint of treatment applications. Observational data on the independent variables indicated that most treatments were being most effectively applied at that time. Some Ss appeared to have had an overdose of biracial interaction by the end of the treatments.

Another variable which had an undetermined effect on the study was the generally tense relationship between blacks and whites in the city in which the study was conducted. One major high school in the city had been closed several times because of race riots, and racial problems in the city had received extensive attention in the local news media. Racial tension in the city finally resulted in a school-wide racial confrontation near the end of the treatment period. The confrontation produced immediate and complete polarization between black and white students. Although a major riot was averted, police occupied the building for more than a week and many white students did not return to school for several days. Some students dropped from school after the confrontation. For example, a white student in the Teacher Reinforcement group who had established significant rapport with several black isolates transferred to another school the week following the confrontation.

A factor which undoubtedly limited the effectiveness of the Peer Reinforcement and Role Modeling treatments was the dearth of potent reinforcers and role models in the respective classes. Only two of the six peer reinforcers consistently exhibited appropriate behavior toward isolates of the opposite race. In the Role Modeling treatment only two models, one black and one white, appeared to have any degree of popularity among members of the opposite race. Although most of the isolates were males, only two of the role models were males.

The effectiveness of treatments, such as those applied in the present study, is markedly delimited by a multitude of variables in the school, community, and society which militate against interracial harmony. For example, in the Role Modeling treatment the same models who dispensed reinforcement within triad sessions consistently failed to instigate cooperative behavior between themselves and the isolates outside the triad. In many cases, cooperative behaviors between the models and the isolates were not only ignored, but were punished by other members of the experimental class. One must admit that the generalizability of treatments like those in the present study will be severely limited without a concomitant increase in reinforcement for interracial cooperation in the environment outside the immediate treatment settings.

E. Summary

The study appraised the effects of five treatment conditions, contingent teacher reinforcement, peer reinforcement, role modeling, group process, and control, on two major dimensions of interracial harmony, biracial sociometric measures, and biracial behavioral interaction. Sixty racial isolates in five racially balanced classes of a metropolitan junior high school served as Ss. A main effect positive change was obtained on both the sociometric and behavioral measures. Differences between groups in amount of change were statistically nonsignificant. However, the raw data indicated that the control group made the least improvement of any treatment group.

References

1. Criswell, J. A sociometric study of race cleavage in the classroom. *Arch. Psychol.,* 1939, 33, 1-83.
2. Horowitz, E. L. The level of attitude toward the Negro. *Arch. Psychol.,* 1936, 28, 1-47.
3. Lombardi, D. Factors affecting change in attitude toward Negroes among high school students. *J. Negro Educ.,* 1963, 32, 129-136.

4. MADSEN, C. H., & MADSEN, C. K. Teaching/Discipline: Behavioral Principles Toward a Positive Approach. Boston, Mass.: Allyn & Bacon, 1970.
5. MEACHAM, M. L., & WIESEN, A. E. Changing Classroom Behavior: A Manual for Precision Teaching. Scranton, Pa.: International Textbook Co., 1970.
6. NEISWORTH, J. T., DENO, S. L., & JENKINS, J. R. Student Motivation and Classroom Management: A Behavioristic Approach. Newark, Del.: Behavior Technics, Inc., 1969.
7. WEBSTER, S. The influence of interracial contact on social acceptance in a newly integrated school. *J. Educ. Psychol.*, 1961, 52, 262-266.
8. WILLIAMS, R. L., & ANANDAM, K. The fallacy of physical desegregation. Unpublished manuscript, The University of Tennessee, Knoxville, 1970.

159

AN EXPERIMENTAL ANALYSIS OF
ANTI-LITTER PROCEDURES[1]

Robert L. Burgess, Roger N. Clark, and John C. Hendee

Traditional approaches to the control of littering in public places usually take one of three forms. One, laws are established imposing sanctions on the behavior. Unfortunately, the difficulty of monitoring littering behavior or even tracing the litter back to its source make successful enforcement of such laws improbable. Two, attempts are made to modify individuals' "attitudes" through advertising campaigns that deplore the ecological and esthetic costs of littering, or extol the virtues of picking up litter. The growing litter problem suggests the ineffectiveness of this approach. Three, attempts are made through survey research to discover the "personality" and social characteristics of litterbugs. The difficulty here is that such knowledge does not immediately provide methods for the control of littering.

The objective of this study was to determine if anti-litter behavior could be developed. The question was, what procedures would increase the frequency of picking up litter?

METHOD
Subjects and Setting

The primary subjects were children who attended the Saturday children's matinees in two neighborhood theaters on 14 different occasions. The seating capacity of Theater 1 is 1500, but for the children's matinees the average attendance was only 160. The seating capacity of Theater 2 is 800, and average attendance was 220.

Procedure

At each performance the audience size was determined from the ticket sales. The usherettes were asked to put all of the litter they collected into a special container, which was not used by anyone else. When the matinee was over, the litter from the trash cans was weighed, and then the floor was swept and that litter weighed. The litter collected from the usherettes' container was weighed along with the litter swept from the floor. The dependent variable was the per cent of the total litter in the theater deposited in the trash cans.

The basic design utilized was the ABA reversibility method (Sidman 1960; Burgess and Bushell 1969). The experimental conditions imposed in Theater 1 were baseline, litterbags, baseline, litterbags plus instructions

[1]This study was financed by the Recreation Research Project of the USDA Forest Service, Pacific Northwest Forest and Range Experiment Station. The authors wish to express appreciation to Mr. Robert Bond of Sterling Recreation Enterprises in Seattle, Mr. James Wolford, Manager of the Lynn-Twin Theater, and Mr. Robert Presley, Manager of the Lewis and Clark Theater. Without their cooperation this study could not have been conducted. We would also like to thank Don Bushell, Jr., for his editorial suggestions.

JOURNAL OF APPLIED BEHAVIOR ANALYSIS, 1971, Vol. 4, pp. 71-75.

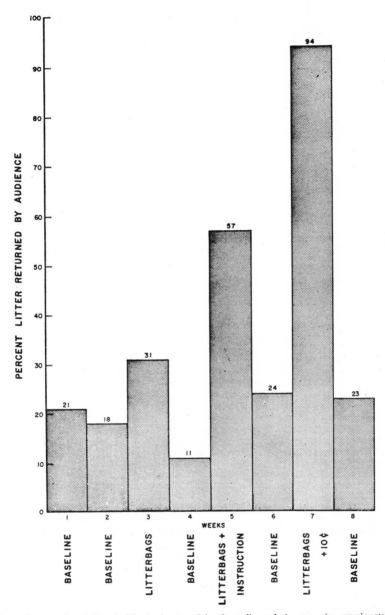

Fig. 1. Per cent of total litter in Theater 1 returned by the audience during successive experimental conditions.

to use them, baseline, litterbags plus 10¢, baseline. The sequence of procedures in Theater 2 was baseline, extra trash cans, litter film, litterbags plus tickets to a movie, baseline.

Baseline. This condition established the amount of litter normally found in the theaters. No special anti-litter procedures were in effect during baseline conditions.

Extra trash cans. This condition was the same as baseline except that the number of trash cans normally present in the theater was doubled. These additional cans were placed more conspicuously than the usual ones.

Litter film. This condition was the same as baseline except that before the regular show an anti-litter film was shown. The film, titled "Litterbug", is a Walt Disney children's cartoon.

Litterbags. A litterbag was given to each person as he entered the theater. As he was handed his litterbag he was told: "This is for you to use while you are in the theater."

Litterbags plus instructions. As in the previous condition, all persons entering the theater were given litterbags. In addition, an announcement was made at intermission in which the audience was instructed to: "Put your trash into the litterbags and put the bag into one of the trash cans in the lobby before leaving the theater."

Litterbags plus 10¢. This condition was exactly the same as the Litterbags condition except that each person was additionally told: "If you bring a bag of litter to the lobby before leaving the theater, you will receive one dime in exchange." Children bringing empty litterbags were told to collect some litter from the floor before they would be given a dime.

Litterbags plus tickets. A litterbag was given to each person entering the theater and, before the movie began and at intermission, it was announced to the audience that: "Each person returning a bag of litter will be given a free ticket to a special children's movie." This special movie was shown the following Wednesday afternoon.

RESULTS

The major results of this study are presented in Fig. 1 and 2. Figure 1 indicates that only 19% of the total litter in Theater 1 was properly disposed of by the audience over the five baseline conditions. Litterbags alone increased

that to 31% and litterbags plus instructions resulted in the return of 57% of the litter. However, by far the largest effect in Theater 1 occurred when 10¢ was paid for each bag of litter turned in. There were 137 individuals in the audience and 95 of them (65%) received such payment. In this condition, 94% of the litter present in the theater was handed in by members of the audience.

In Theater 2, an average of 16% of the litter was placed in trash cans over the three baseline conditions. Doubling the number of trash cans available in the theater produced no effect, and the Disney anti-littering film increased the amount of litter returned only 5% above baseline. In contrast, when members of the audience were given free tickets to a movie upon depositing their litter, 95% of the total litter in the theater was placed in the receptacles. On this day there were 485 people in the audience and 285 of them (59%) received free tickets.

On the following Wednesday, 143 of them attended the special movie. Fifteen of the 143 children attending this special show had not received tickets but were admitted upon the insistence of several irate parents who apparently misunderstood the theater manager's instructions. All of these children came with friends who had received the special ticket. At the completion of this movie, over twice as much litter was turned in by the audience than that obtained during the standard baseline conditions.

DISCUSSION

Several of the procedures employed in this study have a long history of use. For example, some business firms offer free litterbags to their customers, assuming that they will be used. Likewise, the National Park Service and Forest Service commonly offer litterbags and literature to tourists in their respective areas. However, the high level of littering in streets, highways, and in parks and public places suggests that litterbags, if used at all, are employed by only a small percentage of the people. Data from the present study support such a contention. Another common argument is that people would not litter if ample trash receptacles were available. Indeed, a national public opinion survey study of littering concluded that the absence of trash receptacles

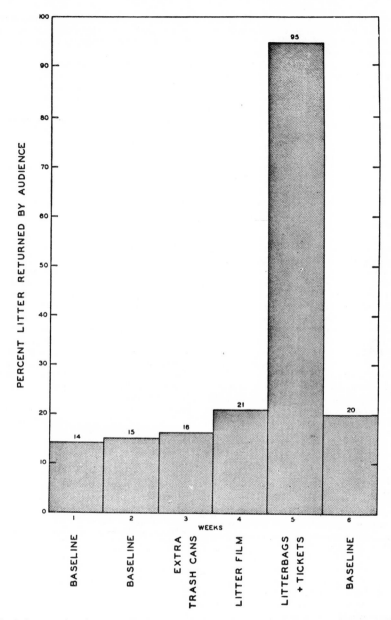

Fig. 2. Per cent of total litter in Theater 2 returned by audience during successive experimental conditions.

was second only to carelessness and indifference as a cause of litter (Keep America Beautiful, 1968). As reasonable as the "absence of trash cans" argument appears, the data from this study suggest otherwise. Doubling the number of trash cans in this study had no effect on littering.

Another common approach to combat littering is through propaganda campaigns designed to change people's presumed "attitudes" toward such behavior. Spot commercials on television exhort people to refrain from littering. Similar attempts are found in billboard announcements and advertisements in newspapers and magazines. Again, data from this study suggest that such attempts may scarcely be worth the effort and cost. The level of litter remained essentially constant after the showing of an anti-litter film.

A similar anti-litter approach is found in posted instructions proscribing littering or appealing for disposal of litter in appropriate receptacles. Examples include signs posted on highways and in public places, as well as anti-litter messages on cans, bottles, and packages. Data from this study suggest that such a tactic might help to alleviate the problem, at least where instructions can be given verbally. However, the study indicates such a solution is only partial since over 40% of the litter was still found on the floor after the audience was instructed to dispose of it.

Data such as these imply a need for alternative approaches to the problem of littering. One alternative is suggested from the experimental analysis of behavior. The following assumptions can be made. First, littering is a member of the more general class of operant behavior. Second, there are some rather immediate consequences of littering that may serve to maintain it at a high level. Carrying of litter is probably for most people aversive. Hence, its quick disposal by dropping it on the floor or ground or by throwing it out of a car window would be negatively reinforced. Third, other consequences, such as defacement of the environment, are more remote and, thereby, exercise much less control over the behavior. Legal sanctions such as fines may have little effect for precisely the same reason. The probability of being detected, arrested, and fined is simply too low and intermittent to control such behavior effectively.

These observations suggest that the level of littering might be reduced if immediate positive consequences contingent on anti-litter behavior could be scheduled. The present data clearly indicate that such a tactic is possible and effective. Using either one dime or a free ticket to another movie as reinforcers increased the total amount of litter returned by the audience to 94 and 95%.

To give the reader some idea of the quantity of litter involved and the consistency of the results regardless of the amount of litter, under the litterbag plus 10¢ condition, a total of 4869 grams of litter was in the theater at the end of the matinee. Of this, 4594 g (94%) were deposited in the trash cans. Under the litterbag plus tickets condition, there were 16,226 g of litter in the theater, of which 15,426 g (95%) were deposited in the receptacles. For comparison, under average baseline conditions one would have expected to find 84% (13,630 g) on the floor and only 16% (2596 g) in the trash cans had the special ticket not been offered. To illustrate further the effectiveness of the anti-litter incentives, the ratio of litter in trash cans to litter on the floor was changed from 1:5 under baseline conditions to 19:1 when free tickets were offered.

In conclusion, this study suggests the possible utility of employing positive reinforcement procedures to combat litter in other areas. Indeed, we are in the process of completing a similar analysis in a campground environment. Preliminary results again indicate the promise of the approach presented in this report. Hopefully, studies such as these will encourage others to carry out experimental analyses of ecological problems.

REFERENCES

Burgess, R. L. and Bushell, Don. *Behavioral sociology: the experimental analysis of social process.* New York: Columbia University Press, 1969. Pp. 145-174.

Keep America Beautiful. *Who litters and why: summary of survey findings concerning public awareness and concern about the problem of litter.* 99 Park Avenue, New York, 1968.

Sidman, M. *Tactics of scientific research: evaluating experimental data in psychology.* New York: Basic Books, 1960. Pp. 110-139.